MONEY

WE MUST content ourselves with that which is within our reach; and that which cannot be approached by logical inference let us leave to him who has been endowed with that great and divine influence, expressed in the words: "Mouth to mouth do I speak with Him."

From Maimonides (1135–1204),
A Guide for the Perplexed

MONEY

SECOND EDITION

LAWRENCE S. RITTER
&
WILLIAM L. SILBER

Basic Books, Inc., Publishers

NEW YORK

FOR

Bella and Irving Ritter

AND

Lillian F. Silber

a mother, a father,

and a wife

all of whom deserve their share

of the blame

Acknowledgment is gratefully made
for permission to reproduce two lines from
Those Were The Days, Gene Raskin.
TRO © 1962, 1968 by Essex Music, Inc.

CONTENTS

PART I

IN THE BEGINNING

1. *A Book for the Curious*   3

2. *All That Glitters*   7
   THE SUPPLY OF MONEY
   THE CENTRAL BANK AND MONEY CREATION
   DOES MONEY MATTER?

3. *Money in Action*   21
   THE MISSING LINK
   LIVING WITH VELOCITY

4. *The Monetarists versus the Keynesians*   29
   THE MONETARIST VIEW
   THE KEYNESIAN VIEW OF MONEY
   WHITHER GOETH THE INTEREST RATE?
   IS IT MONEY OR CREDIT?
   WHO IS RIGHT?

PART II

THE POWER OF THE PURSE

5. *How Effective Is Monetary Policy?*   45

    TIME LAGS IN MONETARY POLICY
    THE IMPACT OF MONETARY POLICY ON GNP
    THE EFFECT OF MONETARY POLICY
       ON INTEREST RATES
    INVESTMENT SPENDING
    STATE AND LOCAL GOVERNMENT SPENDING
       AND CONSUMER SPENDING
    LAGS AGAIN

6. *Is Money the Inflation Culprit?*   59

    TOO MUCH MONEY CHASING TOO FEW GOODS
    CREEPING INFLATION
    DEMAND PULL
    COST PUSH
    MONEY AND CREEPING INFLATION
    THE TRADE-OFF BETWEEN PRICE STABILITY
       AND EMPLOYMENT
    THE MONETARIST CHALLENGE
       TO THE PHILLIPS CURVE
    WAGE-PRICE CONTROLS AND ALL THAT

7. *Are High Interest Rates Always Bad?*   78

    THE CONSPIRATORIAL INTERPRETATION
       OF INTEREST RATES
    THE RICH GET RICHER AND THE POOR
       GET POORER
    DO HIGH INTEREST RATES CREATE
       UNEMPLOYMENT?
    DO HIGH INTEREST RATES MAKE
       INFLATION WORSE?

PART III

FEDERAL RESERVE POLICY-MAKING

8. *Who's in Charge Here?* 91

FORMAL STRUCTURE
THE REALITIES OF POWER
HOW INDEPENDENT THE CENTRAL BANK?

9. *Indicators and Instruments* 104

HOW IMPORTANT IS THE DISCOUNT RATE?
DISCOUNT RATE VERSUS RESERVE REQUIREMENTS
VERSUS OPEN MARKET OPERATIONS
A PRIDE OF LIONS, A GAGGLE OF GEESE,
AND A PLETHORA OF INDICATORS
SOME HELPFUL HINTS

10. *The Nuts and Bolts of Monetary Policy* 120

THE FOMC DIRECTIVE
CHANGED EMPHASIS IN THE DIRECTIVE
THE OPERATING ROOM

11. *Should a Robot Replace the Federal Reserve?* 132

RULES VERSUS DISCRETION

PART IV

FISCAL POLICY

12. *Fiscal Policy versus Monetary Policy* 139

HOW FISCAL POLICY WORKS
MEASURING FISCAL POLICY
FINANCIAL ASPECTS OF FISCAL POLICY
THE MONETARISTS VERSUS THE KEYNESIANS

PART V

OF BONDS, STOCKS, AND INTERMEDIARIES

13. *Should We Worry about the National Debt?*   157

    THE NATIONAL DEBT EQUALS
    THE NATIONAL CREDIT
    THE REAL BURDEN OF THE DEBT: I
    THE REAL BURDEN OF THE DEBT: II
    THE NUTS AND BOLTS OF DEBT MANAGEMENT

14. *Does Monetary Policy Affect the Stock Market?* 170

    A MONEY SUPPLY VIEW OF STOCK PRICES
    MONETARY POLICY AND WALL STREET

15. *What Is Financial Intermediation?*   182

    FINANCIAL INTERMEDIATION LOWERS
      INTEREST RATES
    INTERMEDIATION AND MONETARY POLICY
    DISINTERMEDIATION
    DEPOSIT RATE CEILINGS

16. *The Structure of the Commercial
    Banking Industry*   196

    DEPOSIT RATE CEILINGS AGAIN
    BRANCHING AND NEW ENTRY
    DO THE GIANT BANKS POSE
      A MONOPOLY THREAT?

PART VI

MONEY AND NATIONAL PRIORITIES

17. *Financial Resources, Real Resources,
    and National Priorities*   207

    QUANTIFYING REORDERED PRIORITIES
    PEACE AND GROWTH DIVIDENDS
    DELIBERATE RESOURCE REALLOCATION

REORDERED PRIORITIES MEAN HIGHER TAXES
CAN SELECTIVE CREDIT CONTROLS HELP?
A CATECHISM ON SELECTIVE CREDIT POLICIES

18. *Does Tight Money Discriminate against Housing?*   221

     THE TRUTH ABOUT HOUSING
     THE INSTABILITY OF SUPPLY
     THE SENSITIVITY OF DEMAND
     FANNY MAE AND HER FRIENDS

PART VII

INTERNATIONAL FINANCE

19. *Money in International Finance*   233

     THE DISCIPLINE OF THE BALANCE OF PAYMENTS
     FLOATING EXCHANGE RATES

20. *International Financial Crises*   241

     THE GENESIS OF INTERNATIONAL
       MONETARY CRISES
     THE SPECIAL CASE OF THE UNITED STATES
     WHY DID DOLLAR DEVALUATION TAKE SO LONG?
     DOMESTIC COMPLICATIONS
     THE REAL STORM

21. *What about Gold?*   259

     GOLD AT HOME
     GOLD ABROAD: INTERNATIONAL LIQUIDITY
     PAPER GOLD?

EPILOGUE

22. *Is Money Becoming Obsolete?*   275

     THE DECLINE OF DEMAND DEPOSITS
     DEBITS AND CREDITS IN THE YEAR 2000

IMPLICATIONS FOR FINANCIAL MARKETS
IMPLICATIONS FOR THE ECONOMY

Selected Readings   282

Index   285

PART I
In the Beginning

1

A BOOK FOR THE CURIOUS

In 1931, Babe Ruth received a salary of $80,000 from the New York Yankees. In 1972, Henry Aaron was paid a reported $200,000 by the Atlanta Braves. Who was better off?

After income taxes, Ruth's take-home pay was $68,500, while Aaron wound up with $78,000. However, consumer prices in 1972 were about three times higher than in 1931; at those prices, Aaron's $78,000 could buy only what $26,000 would have bought in 1931. Compare the Babe's $68,500 with Aaron's $26,000: Ruth's salary, in terms of post-tax purchasing power, was worth considerably more than double Bad Henry's. (He's called Bad Henry because he's so good.)

Much of this differential in Ruth's favor is clearly due to today's higher tax rates. But regardless of taxes, the Babe was better off. Aaron's $200,000 can buy only the real goods and services that $67,000 could purchase in 1931, since prices are now three times higher. So even forgetting about taxes, Babe Ruth's real income was about 20 percent larger than Aaron's—$80,000 compared with $67,000.

All of which is not meant to prove that Babe Ruth was a better baseball player than Hank Aaron (which he was), but that inflation distorts economic relationships. Hank

Aaron will make do, inflation or no inflation, but for most people rising prices are a more painful matter. As your income goes up, you may think you are earning more and moving up the ladder, but if prices are rising faster it is a mirage. You may be earning more dollars, but each dollar is worth less and less, so that after all is said and done you are no better off (and maybe worse) than you were before.

What does all this have to do with money? It is widely believed that increases in the price level are synonymous with increases in the money supply. The reason for this book is to explore precisely and thoroughly the influence of money on the economy. How it affects the price level, what it does to the volume of employment, whether it enhances or inhibits economic growth, and what role it plays in the attainment of national priorities. In short, this is a book about money and monetary policy.

Other questions also spring to mind. Is money responsible for the ups and downs of stock prices? Why is the housing industry apparently so susceptible to changes in monetary policy? Is gold an essential part of our monetary system or a vestigial remnant of bygone days? Why did we devalue the dollar?

These questions have been highlighted in recent years by the rebirth of monetary policy as an instrument of national economic policy, and also by widely publicized debates between the Monetarists (remember Milton Friedman?) and the Keynesians (if you have forgotten who John Maynard Keynes was, Paul Samuelson will do). The Monetarists are the standard-bearers of monetary policy and the Keynesians the champions of fiscal policy. In recent years, for example, great controversy arose between them as to whether inflation could best be stopped by exclusive reliance on monetary policy or by increased taxes, a tool of fiscal policy.

We will explore the intricacies of money and monetary policy in the following way. Part I lays the foundations for understanding problems of the sort we have mentioned above. In particular, Chapters 2 and 3 deal with the essentials of money and its relationship to the overall economy, and Chapter 4 with the crucial debate between the Monetarists and the Keynesians. How does this theoretical confrontation lead to alternative policy recommendations for solving real-world problems?

Against this background, Part II examines, in detail, the impact of monetary policy on the economy. How does it work? What effect does it have on the price level? What are some of the implications of high interest rates? Part III, in the same vein, explores the execution of monetary policy, including the mechanics of who pushes which levers at what times. How can an outsider tell which levers are being pushed? Is there a better way to go about the whole business?

Having explored the execution and the effects of monetary policy, we return in Part IV to the controversy between the Monetarists and the Keynesians, this time concentrating on the potentialities of fiscal policy. Is the policy split in the real world as deep as the ideological chasm that appears to separate Milton Friedman from Paul Samuelson?

Part V takes an in-depth look at a number of puzzling issues that swirl in the wake of both monetary and fiscal policy. Should the national debt rank so high on the Worry Meter scale? Can knowledge of the intricacies of monetary policy help in forecasting the stock market? What is meant by financial intermediation and disintermediation?

Parts VI and VII explore two areas that have attracted widespread attention recently: national priorities and international finance (exchange rates, balance of payments deficits, gold, devaluation, and all that). It is said that only two men in the whole world really understand what international finance is all about—and they disagree. Finally, we end up with our crystal ball and try to fathom what money and the financial system might look like in the Brave New World of the twenty-first century.

This is not a long book. Perhaps it is even too short to do full justice to the gound it covers. Nevertheless, after you finish it, we hope you will be more informed about money and its role in economic life, and more capable of satisfying your curiosity about what is happening today and what is likely to happen tomorrow in the sphinx-like world of monetary policy.

2

ALL THAT GLITTERS

Not too many years ago—say forty-five or so—no one would have thought of writing a book about monetary policy. Who needed it? Money, as everyone knew, depended on gold. And the economy, as everyone also knew, depended on itself. Monetary policy was unnecessary and irrelevant. Not to mention irreverent. Flanked by the twin eternal verities—the gold standard and the balanced budget—laissez-faire reigned supreme.

Back then it was generally assumed that aggregate spending on the nation's output of new goods and services —the economy's gross national product (GNP)—might occasionally fluctuate somewhat. However, it was expected that such fluctuations in spending and GNP would be moderate and not too disturbing, provided the government maintained the gold standard, balanced the budget, and thereafter kept out of the way. The economy, it was widely believed, was *inherently* stable. Left alone, it would automatically generate the right amount of spending to produce full employment, stable prices, a high rate of economic growth, balance in international payments . . . and almost anything else you might like to add to the list.

> Those were the days, my friend,
> We thought they'd never end.

But end they did. There are still some whose faith in the eternal verities remains pure and unshaken; Roosevelt's finagling is to blame for the Great Depression and his abandonment of gold is responsible for the subsequent inflation. For most people, however, the issue now is not *whether* the government should intervene—but how, when, and to what extent.

The means that are most frequently used today are monetary policy (the subject of this book) and fiscal policy. The ends are not particularly new—high employment, price stability, economic growth, and balance-of-payments equilibrium—but the means are. Do the ends justify the means? Are the means capable of achieving the ends?

Very few people still equate paper money with rampant inflation, unbalanced budgets with creeping socialism, and Keynes with Marx. But the emotional content of the argument has not disappeared. It has merely moved next door —to the debate between the Monetarists and the Keynesians, between monetary policy versus fiscal policy, and to controversy over the execution of monetary policy.

As a first approximation, monetary policy is concerned with regulating the money supply in order to achieve the goals of national economic policy. Similarly, fiscal policy deals with changes in government spending and tax rates for the same purposes. We will return to fiscal policy later in the book. First, however, let us set the framework for our main concern—money and monetary policy.

The Supply of Money

How large a money supply should we have in the United States? What, in fact, do we mean by the term *money* to begin with?

Money is whatever is generally accepted as a means of payment or in settlement of debts. The Indians used beads, the Eskimos used fishhooks, and we use checks and currency. On that basis, the money supply in this country amounts to over $230 billion, more than $180 billion in demand deposits (checking accounts) at commercial banks and about $50 billion in currency (bills and coins).

A few economists, notably Milton Friedman, also include savings deposits at commercial banks in the money supply. He argues that while a savings deposit cannot be used directly as a means of payment, since checks cannot be written on it, such deposits are so easily converted into cash that they should be counted as money. If we do add savings deposits at commercial banks, the money supply more than doubles, to nearly $500 billion. On similar grounds, other economists include deposits at mutual savings banks and deposits (usually called shares) in savings and loan associations as well, which would add another $250 billion to make a grand total of $750 billion.

However, most economists prefer the narrow definition of the money supply, simply the $230 billion of demand deposits and currency, because that and only that is what is generally accepted as a means of payment. Throughout this book we will use this definition. Now that we know what money is, the question still remains: how much of it should there be?

In theory, the answer is simple enough; we should have enough money so that we buy, at current prices, all the goods and services the economy is able to turn out. If we spend less, we will have idle capacity and idle men. If we spend more, we will wind up with higher prices but no more real goods or services. We need a money supply, in other words, that is large enough to generate sufficient spending to produce full employment at stable prices. Less spending would mean recession and more would mean inflation.

In practice, however, the answer is not quite so simple. Precisely how much money will give us that appropriate volume of spending? The answer is not clear, because any given amount of money can conceivably be spent more or less rapidly, thereby generating a rather wide range of potential spending. In brief, the velocity of money, its rate of turnover, is as important as the supply. It is so important, in fact, that we will devote all of the next chapter to velocity and its implications.

Where, in all of this, does gold fit in? The amount of gold in the country is only about $10 billion. With that little gold, how do we get $230 billion of money? Not too difficult—we just create it out of thin air under governmental supervision. In 1968, the last remaining link between the money supply and gold was severed, when the law requiring a 25 percent gold backing behind most of our currency was repealed. If that is all news to you, it is a good indication of just how unimportant the connection between gold and money has always been, at least in our lifetime.

Both demand deposits and currency can be increased (or decreased) without any relation whatsoever to gold. Does that disturb you? Does it lead you to distrust the value of your money? Then send it to us. We will be delighted to pay you ninety cents on the dollar, which should be a bargain if you believe all you read about a dollar being worth only fifty-seven cents, or forty-three cents, or whatever the latest figure might be.

If gold is not the watchdog, what is? What supervision is there over the creation (and destruction) of money? In other words, who controls and formulates monetary policy?

The Central Bank and Money Creation

The monetary authority in most countries is called the central bank. A central bank does not deal directly with the public; it is rather a bank for banks, and it is responsible for the execution of national monetary policy. In the United States the central bank is the Federal Reserve System, created by Congress in 1913. It consists of twelve district Federal Reserve banks, scattered throughout the country, and a board of governors in Washington. This hydra-headed monster, which some view as benign but others consider an ever-lurking peril, possesses ultimate authority over the money supply.

As noted above, the money supply consists of currency and checking accounts. Currency is manufactured by money factories—the Bureau of Engraving and Printing and the Mint—and then shipped under rather heavy guard to the Treasury and the Federal Reserve for further distribution. For the most part it enters circulation when people and business firms cash checks at their local banks. Thus it is the public that ultimately decides what proportion of the money supply will be in the form of currency, with the Federal Reserve banks wholesaling the necessary coins and paper to local banks. The Federal Reserve is not particularly concerned with the fraction of the money supply that is in one form or another, but rather with the *total* of demand deposits plus currency.

Money that is in the form of demand deposits, and that is three-quarters of it, comes into being when commercial banks extend credit—that is, when they make loans or buy securities. It vanishes, as silently as it came, when banks contract credit—when bank loans are repaid or banks sell securities. It is precisely here, through its ability to control the behavior of commercial banks, that the Federal Reserve wields its primary authority over the money supply and thereby implements monetary policy. This process of money creation by the banks under the influence of the Federal Reserve is sufficiently important and complex to deserve further explanation.

When a bank makes a loan to a consumer or business firm, it typically creates a checking account for the borrower's use. For example, when you borrow $1,000 from your friendly neighborhood bank, the bank will take your IOU and give you a checking account in return. From the commercial bank's point of view, it has an additional $1,000 of assets (namely, your IOU); this is matched by an additional $1,000 of liabilities (namely, your checking account). You could, of course, ask for $1,000 in $10 bills right then and there, stuff them in your wallet, and depart. But more likely you would be equally satisfied with the demand deposit, because by writing checks on it you can make payments just as well as with currency. The creation of this $1,000 in bank demand deposits means that the money supply has increased by $1,000.

Similarly, when a bank buys a corporate or government bond, it pays for it by opening a checking account for the seller. Assume you are holding a $1,000 corporate or government bond in your investment portfolio, and you need cash. You might sell the bond to your local bank, which would then add $1,000 to your checking account. Once again, from the point of view of the bank, its assets (bonds) and liabilities (demand deposits) have gone up by $1,000. Just as by a bank loan, money has been created; the supply of money in the economy has increased by $1,000.

Conversely, when you repay a bank loan, the bank gives you back your IOU and at the same time lowers your demand deposit balance. If a bank sells a bond to an individual, the same reduction in demand deposits occurs. The supply of money declines. To repeat: banks create money (demand deposits) when they lend or buy securities and destroy money when their loans are repaid or they sell securities.

Can they do this without limit? Is there any control over their ability to create and destroy money? No they can't and yes there is, and that is where the Federal Reserve comes into the picture.

A commercial bank cannot always expand its demand deposit liabilities by making loans or buying securities. Commercial banks that are members of the Federal Reserve System, and they include those that do most of the banking business, must hold reserves against their demand deposit liabilities—the current requirement is reserves of about 15 percent against demand deposits. *These reserves must be held in the form of vault cash or as a deposit in their regional Federal Reserve Bank.* Therefore, only if a commercial bank has "excess" reserves, reserves over and above its requirements, can it create new demand deposits by making loans and buying securities. Once a bank is "loaned up," with no more excess reserves, its ability to create money ceases. And if it has deficient reserves, not enough to support its existing deposits, the bank must somehow get additional reserves. Otherwise, it has no choice but to call in loans or sell securities in order to bring its deposits back in line with its reserves. If a bank has demand deposits of $10,000 but only $1,400 in reserves, it would be $100 short of meeting its required reserves. One way to set itself right with the Federal Reserve would be to call in $667 worth of loans. This would reduce its demand deposits to $9,333, at which level its $1,400 of reserves satisfies the legal 15 percent requirement.

It is through the fulcrum of these reserves that the Federal Reserve influences commercial bank lending and investing and thereby the money supply. The Federal Reserve manipulates the reserves of the banking system and the amount of demand deposits that they can support in several different ways.

In the first place, within prescribed limits established by Congress, the Federal Reserve can specify the reserve requirement percentage. Lowering the percentage, say from 15 to 10 percent, will instantly and automatically increase banks' excess reserves, enabling banks to make more loans (or buy securities) and to expand demand deposits. If reserve requirements were lowered from 15 to 10 percent, the bank with the $100 reserve deficiency would suddenly find itself with $400 in excess reserves. Raising the percentage, say to 20 percent, will just as quickly reduce excess reserves or create deficiencies, pressuring banks to call in loans (or sell securities), thereby reducing demand deposits.

Second, through facilities available for "discounting," member banks can temporarily borrow reserves from their regional Federal Reserve Bank at a price (the discount rate). For example, the problem bank, with demand deposits of $10,000 but only $1,400 in reserves, could avoid the embarrassment of having to call in loans if it were willing to borrow the needed $100 in reserves from its regional Federal Reserve Bank. The ability to borrow these reserves means that the money supply can remain unchanged. A bank could also take the initiative and borrow additional reserves to make *new* loans and thereby *increase* the money supply. The Federal Reserve influences the willingness of banks to borrow reserves by manipulating the rate it charges on such loans. A lower discount rate will tend to make borrowing reserves more attractive to the commercial banks, and a higher rate will tend to make it less attractive.

Third, and most important of all as a means of day-to-day policy-making, the Federal Reserve can buy or sell government securities (open market operations), thereby enlarging or diminishing bank reserves. About $175 billion worth of marketable government securities are held as investments by the public—by individuals, corporations, financial institutions, and so on. These government securities came into being when the United States Treasury had to borrow to finance past budget deficits. Some are long-term bonds, running twenty or thirty years until maturity, and others are shorter term, all the way down to government securities that are issued for only a few months, called Treasury bills. The existence of this pool of widely held marketable securities, with many potential buyers and sellers, offers an ideal vehicle through which the Federal Reserve can affect bank reserves.

When the Federal Reserve *buys* government securities in the open market, much as you would buy a stock or a bond on one of the stock exchanges, it pays for them with a check drawn on itself; when the seller deposits that check in a commercial bank, the bank's deposits at the Federal Reserve Bank—its reserves—increase. With more reserves, the bank can make loans and increase its demand deposits.

Take the following concrete example. When the Federal Reserve buys $1,000 in government securities from an insurance company (or from any individual, for that matter), it pays the insurance company with a $1,000 check drawn on itself. When the insurance company deposits the check in its commercial bank, a demand deposit of $1,000 is created for it, and the bank now has the Federal Reserve's check as an asset. This bank, in turn, presents the check for payment at its local Federal Reserve Bank and receives in exchange reserves equal to $1,000, the amount of the check. So far, the money supply has gone up by $1,000, and the bank has additional reserves. On the basis of these additional reserves, the banking system can now create *more* demand deposits by making new loans.

But what the central bank giveth the central bank can taketh away. If the Federal Reserve *sells* government securities out of its portfolio, it *receives* a check for them, drawn on some commercial bank; the Federal Reserve collects by reducing that bank's deposit at the Federal Reserve Bank, thus diminishing the bank's reserves. Result: both the money supply and bank reserves fall.

Note that the Federal Reserve could achieve the same ends—that is, change the money supply and bank reserves —by buying or selling any financial asset, any type of bond or stock. The reason for limiting its open market operations to the purchase and sale of government securities is quite obvious; who would determine whether the Federal Reserve should buy General Motors stock or IBM? The Federal Reserve is smart enough, at least in this respect, to keep its hands out of the public hair.

To summarize: these techniques—setting reserve requirements, varying the discount rate, and open market operations—put the reserves of the commercial banking system (and their demand deposit potential) pretty tightly under the control of the Federal Reserve, thereby giving it sufficient leverage with which to control the money supply.

But does it really matter? What difference does it make whether the money supply increases or decreases?

Does Money Matter?

We have come full circle, back to the question that started us off: how much money should we have in the United States? What effects does monetary policy have on the economy?

Monetary policy consists of varying the amount of money in the economy, presumably increasing it (or, more realistically, increasing the rate at which it is growing) during a recession in order to encourage spending, and decreasing it (or at least increasing it at less than the normal rate) during a boom in order to inhibit spending. But whether just changing the money supply really does influence people's spending is not immediately that obvious.

Many appear to believe that monetary policy affects people's wealth and in that fashion influences their spending. Clearly, if people have more money and less of nothing else, they are wealthier and will probably spend more. But *pure* monetary policy—that is, monetary policy alone, without any accompanying fiscal policy (such as a budget deficit)—usually does not alter people's wealth *directly*.

An expansion in the money supply via pure monetary policy, for example, does not increase wealth directly, because the public gives up an asset or incurs a liability as part of the very process through which currency or demand deposits rise. If the money supply is increased by Federal Reserve open market purchases of securities, the increased demand deposit acquired by the public is offset by the reduction in its holdings of government securities (they were purchased by the Federal Reserve). In any subsequent expansion of demand deposits by bank lending or security purchases, the public acquires an asset (demand deposits) but either creates a liability against itself in the

form of a bank loan or sells to the bank an asset of equal
value, such as a government bond.

What a change in the money supply *does* do directly is
alter the *liquidity* of the public. Money is the most liquid of
all assets. A liquid asset is something that can be turned
into cash—that is, can be sold or "liquidated"—quickly,
with no loss in dollar value. Money already *is* cash. You
can't get more liquid than that!

Since monetary policy by itself *can* alter the liquidity of
the public's portfolio of total assets—including, in that
balance sheet, holdings of real as well as financial assets—
it should thereby lead to portfolio readjustments that involve spending decisions. An increase in the money supply
implies that the public is more liquid than formerly; a decrease in the money supply implies that the public is less
liquid than before. If the public was satisfied with its
previous holdings of money relative to the rest of its assets,
now that it has more money there will presumably be
readjustments throughout the rest of its portfolio.

In other words, these changes in liquidity should lead to
more (or less) spending on either real assets (cars and
television sets) or financial assets (stocks and bonds). If
spending on real assets expands, this means an increased
demand for goods and services and GNP is directly
affected. If spending on financial assets goes up, the increased demand for stocks and bonds drives up securities
prices. Higher securities prices mean lower interest rates.*

* To avoid falling into the well-known Galbraithian footnote phobia
("No footnotes are sillier than footnotes"—John Kenneth Galbraith,
The Great Crash [Boston: Houghton Mifflin, 1961], p. xxiii), we hereby
offer our one and only:

Since it comes up again and again, it is worth devoting a moment to
the *inverse* relationship between the *price* of an income-earning asset
and its effective *rate of interest* (or yield). For example, a long-term
bond that carries a fixed interest income of $10 a year, and costs $100,
yields an annual interest rate of 10 percent. However, if the price of

The fall in interest rates may induce more spending on housing and on plant and equipment (investment spending), thereby influencing GNP through that route.

At this point, it is worth noting that while monetary policy does not alter wealth directly, it does have an indirect wealth effect through its impact on interest rates and securities prices. Lower interest rates mean higher securities prices, and higher interest rates mean lower securities prices. Capital losses are familiar to us all, and perhaps capital gains as well—even if only on paper. Such changes in the values of stocks and bonds in an individual's portfolio may very well alter spending on real goods (a new home) or even on real bads (pornography). This indirect wealth effect provides another link between monetary policy and GNP.

At the root of the effectiveness of monetary policy, however, is still its initial impact on the liquidity of the public. And whether a change in the supply of liquidity actually does influence spending or not depends on what is happening to the demand for liquidity. If the supply of money is increased but the demand for money expands even more, the additional money will be held and not spent. "Easy" or "tight" money is not really a matter of increases or decreases in the money supply in an absolute sense; rather, it is increases or decreases relative to the demand for money. Indeed, changes in monetary policy are most often couched in terms of increases or decreases in the rate of growth of money, rather than in terms of absolute changes. In the

---

the bond were to rise to $200, the effective rate of interest would drop to 10/200 or 5 percent. And if the price of the security were to fall to $50, the yield would rise to 10/50 or 20 percent. Conclusion: a rise (or fall) in the price of a bond is reflected, in terms of sheer arithmetic, in an automatic change in the opposite direction in the effective rate of interest. To say the price of bonds rose or the rate of interest fell are but two different ways of saying the same thing.

past decade, we have had few periods in which the money supply actually decreased, yet we have had many periods of tight money because the rate of growth was so small that the demand for money rose faster than the supply.

The question of changes in the supply of money relative to the demand for it returns us once again to the speed with which money is spent, its rate of turnover or velocity, the subject of the following chapter. In subsequent chapters, we shall delve deeper into the influence of money and monetary policy on the economy—including interest rate effects, wealth effects, and maybe even a few special effects.

3

MONEY IN ACTION

When the Federal Reserve increases the money supply by $1 billion, how does it know how much of an effect this will have on people's spending and thereby on GNP? Say we are in a recession, with GNP $20 billion below prosperity levels. Can the Federal Reserve induce a $20 billion expansion in spending by increasing the money supply by $2 billion? Or will it take a $10 billion . . . or a $15 billion . . . increase in the money supply to do the job? If people always respond in a consistent manner to an increase in their liquidity (the proportion of money in their portfolio), the Federal Reserve will be able to gauge the impact on GNP of a change in the money supply. But if people's spending reactions vary unpredictably when there is a change in the money supply, the central bank will never know whether it should alter the money supply a little or a lot (or even at all!) to bring about a specified change in spending.

Clearly, this is the key puzzle the Federal Reserve must solve if it is to operate effectively. After all, the central bank is not in business to change the money supply just for the sake of changing the money supply. Money is only a means to an end, and the end is the total volume of spending (GNP); when the chips are down, GNP will determine whether the overall economy is performing well or poorly.

How stable is the public's propensity to spend on goods and services out of increased liquidity? Does the public react to a change in the money supply predictably enough to allow the central bank to calculate the effect of its actions on GNP? Or is the reaction so unpredictable that the Federal Reserve can do no more than probe and pray?

The Missing Link

When the money supply increases, the recipients of this additional liquidity probably spend some of it on goods and services, increasing GNP. The funds thereby move from the original recipients to the sellers of the goods and services. Now *they* have more money than before, and if they behave the same way as the others, they too are likely to spend some of it. GNP thus rises further—and at the same time the money moves on to a still different set of owners who, in turn, may also spend part of it, thereby increasing GNP again.

Over a period of time, say a year, a multiple increase in spending and GNP could thus flow from the initial increase in the stock of money. Whether this expansion in GNP is large or small, relative to the change in the money supply that set it going initially, depends on two things: first, on how much of the new money is respent (passed on) at each stage; and second, on how quickly the respending takes place. If a large fraction of the increased money is respent by each recipient soon after he receives it, GNP will expand a great deal relative to the increase in the stock of money. On the other hand, if a small fraction (or none) of the increased money is respent, or if it is held a long time at each stage, the expansion in GNP during the year will be quite small relative to the enlarged money supply.

This relationship between the increase in GNP over a period of time and the change in the money supply that brought it about is important enough to have a name: the velocity of money. Technically speaking, it is found, after the process has ended, by dividing the total increase in GNP by the increase in the money supply that started it all.

We similarly can compute the velocity of the *total* amount of money in the country by dividing total GNP (not just the increase in it) by the total money supply. This gives us the average number of times each dollar turns over to buy goods and services during the year. In 1971, for example, with a GNP of $1,050 billion and a money supply of $213 billion, the velocity of money was 1,050 divided by 213, or 4.93 per annum. Each dollar, on the average, was spent almost 5 times in purchasing goods and services during 1971.

With this missing link—velocity—now in place, we can reformulate the problem of the Federal Reserve more succinctly. The Federal Reserve controls the supply of money. Its main job is to regulate the flow of spending. The flow of spending, however, depends not only on the supply of money but also on that supply's rate of turnover, or velocity, and this the Federal Reserve does *not* have under its thumb. Since any given supply of money might be spent faster or slower—that is, velocity might rise or fall—a rather wide range of potential spending could conceivably flow from any given stock of money.

The *ideal* situation for the central bank is a stable velocity, or at least one that is changing slowly and predictably over a period of time. If velocity is stable or predictable, or close to it, the Federal Reserve can induce almost any volume of spending it wants simply by adjusting the money supply to the known velocity. For example, the velocity of the total money supply is now about 5. If an *addition* to the money supply also turns over 5 times a year in the purchase of goods and services, then the Federal Reserve knows for sure that if it increases the money supply by a billion dollars the end result will be an increase in GNP of $5 billion. In that case, the Federal Reserve has it made; monetary policy alone would be both necessary *and sufficient* to control aggregate spending.

At the other extreme, the *worst* situation from the point of view of the monetary authorities is if velocity fluctuates randomly or perversely. If velocity moves randomly, up and down without rhyme or reason, it would be impossible to gauge the impact on GNP that might result from a change in the money supply. If movements in velocity are perverse, that would mean that every time the Federal Reserve increased the money supply by 10 percent, velocity would respond by falling 10 percent. Monetary policy would be impotent. Changes in the money supply would merely be offset by an opposite change in velocity, leaving spending (and therefore GNP) unaltered. The public would not be responding to changes in liquidity and would be deciding by itself how much it would spend, irrespective of the actions of the Federal Reserve. Under such circumstances, monetary policy would be close to useless as a tool of national economic policy.

Living with Velocity

The facts are that velocity is neither perfectly stable or fully predictable. Unfortunately for the Federal Reserve, it does not operate in a world designed for its own convenience. With a money supply of $230 billion today, a miscalculation of only 0.1 in velocity means a $23 billion swing in GNP. But all is not necessarily lost. While velocity is not fixed, neither do its movements appear to be random or perverse. If the Federal Reserve could discover the underlying determinants of fluctuations in velocity, it might still be able to coexist with such a moving target.

With that in mind, examining the past may provide a clue to developments in the future. The velocity of the total money supply reached an annual peak of 4 in 1919, when GNP was $80 billion and the money supply $20 billion. It fell slightly during most of the 1920s and then regained that peak of 4 in 1929. Thereafter, during the Depression and World War II, velocity fell almost continuously to an all-time low of 2 in 1946. In that year GNP was about $210 billion and the money supply $105 billion; each dollar, on the average, was being spent only twice.

Since then, however, velocity has risen considerably. It rose to 2.5 by 1950 . . . to 3 by 1955 . . . 3.5 in 1960 . . . reached 4 (the previous peak) in 1964 . . . continued on upward, beyond its previous peak, to 4.5 in 1967 . . . and now it is approaching an annual rate of turnover of 5. The increase since World War II has been steady and even, with only slight dips now and then, usually in recessions, to interrupt an otherwise unbroken upward climb.

But, of course, facts alone do not speak for themselves. Understanding requires interpretation. Why has velocity behaved this way, especially in the past quarter century? After the war it was generally expected that velocity would accelerate somewhat. Unexpected, however, has been the magnitude of the increase and its duration.

Perhaps the main reason for the extent of the postwar

rise in velocity has been the increasing attractiveness of financial assets *other than money*—bonds as well as stocks, savings and loan shares as well as savings accounts in commercial banks—as prudent and desirable outlets in which to invest excess cash. These assets are often highly liquid, almost as liquid as money, and yet they possess an attribute money lacks—the right to receive an interest income. Attractive yields on financial assets other than money have led more and more people to wonder why they should ever hold any idle cash aside from what they need for day-to-day transactions purposes. And traditional concepts about how much cash on hand is really necessary for doing business have also come under reexamination. If cash for day-to-day transactions purposes can be pared down, then some of it can be loaned out to earn interest. The money that is put to work earning interest moves to borrowers who can use it for current purchases. As a result, a larger volume of current spending flows from the same stock of money.

Corporate treasurers, in particular, have found that it pays dividends to scrutinize their cash holdings intensively. Could they manage to get along with somewhat less in the till than they had previously thought of as "normal," and invest a portion in high-yielding time deposits at commercial banks or in U.S. treasury bills (short-term government securities)? Increasingly, the answer has been "yes," and imaginative new techniques of cash management have been developed to facilitate the process (also some not so imaginative old techniques, such as becoming "slow payers" when bills come due).

Nor has this trend escaped the attention of consumers. They have learned to economize on money by substituting lines of credit at retail stores and financial institutions in place of cash reserves; in addition, the growing use of credit cards has drastically reduced household needs for day-to-day transactions money. What was formerly held in the form of non-interest-bearing demand deposits or currency, for emergency use or for current payments, now shifts to interest-bearing savings deposits.

In conclusion, it is clear that velocity has not been stable; however, neither has it fluctuated randomly or perversely. There is a discernible pattern in the movements of velocity during the postwar period—a persistent long-run rise with minor short-run dips during recessions. Even though we may not be able to pinpoint all the specific determinants, we can still see broad cause-and-effect relationships.

Higher interest rates clearly lead to an increase in velocity by inducing business firms and households to economize on money. They hold less, lend out the excess, and others (the borrowers) can then spend it. Once learned, techniques of cash management are not easily forgotten, so that even in recessions, when interest rates fall, velocity does not drop back very far.

Furthermore, the long-run upward trend in velocity over the past quarter century suggests that fundamental structural relationships between the money supply and the spending habits of the community are apparently in the process of transition. New payment methods are developing (credit cards are a prime example), as financial innovation occurs side by side with technological innovation in industry. Such financial innovation, however, rarely takes root overnight. Established payment habits are likely to change only gradually over time.

Thus, although velocity is not fixed, neither is it likely to change drastically in the short run. The Federal Reserve may be able to live with it, even though it is a moving target. By gaining further insight into what makes velocity move, the central bank can establish a range of probabilities as to where velocity is likely to be tomorrow and the day after, and act on that basis. In other words, a morning line on velocity (not unlike the one your local bookie puts out on the races at Hialeah)—provided the odds are unemotionally calculated and continuously reassessed in the light of emerging evidence—might still enable the Federal Reserve to come out a winner.

4

THE MONETARISTS VERSUS

THE KEYNESIANS

Each baby girl and tiny man
That's born into a family nest
Is either a little Keynesian
Or else a little Monetarest.

At an economics conference in the late 1960s, Robert
Solow, a prominent Keynesian from MIT, commented as
follows on a paper presented by Milton Friedman: "Another difference between Milton and myself is that everything reminds Milton of the money supply; well, everything reminds me of sex, but I try to keep it out of my
papers."

Monetarists do, in fact, make so much of the money
supply that they are rather easy to caricature. It appears
frequently in their professional papers circulated among
economists; it figures prominently in their policy recommendations to the government; and some have even shown
how it can make money in the stock market. But so far, at
least, no evidence has been presented on its qualifications
as an aphrodisiac. Don't, however, rule out the possibility.

The president of the United States will use very different
approaches in economic policy-making depending on

whether his orientation is Keynesian or Monetarist. As a Keynesian, he and the chairman of his Council of Economic Advisers would spend considerable time pressing the Congress for countercyclical tax and expenditure legislation. If he were a Monetarist, he would expend more effort trying to influence the actions of the Federal Reserve. The Eisenhower administration had essentially a Monetarist course, while the orientation of economic policy under Kennedy and Johnson was primarily Keynesian. The Nixon administration has used a little bit of everything.

What are the underlying differences between these two schools? And how do their theoretical disputes affect their policy recommendations?

The Monetarist View

The Monetarists used to be called Quantity Theorists. Their lineage can be traced at least as far back as Jean Bodin in the sixteenth century, through John Locke, David Hume, David Ricardo, John Stuart Mill, up to Irving Fisher in the 1920s and 1930s, and now Milton Friedman in the 1960s and 1970s. Historically, they used to be concerned primarily with the relationship between the quantity of money and prices, viewing the money supply as the main determinant of the price level. The modern Quantity Theorists—or Monetarists—no longer believe changes in the money supply affect only the price level. As they see it, the role of money is much broader than that; it is the crucial determinant of GNP.

According to the Monetarists, there is a direct and reliable link between the money supply and GNP. That link is the stability of monetary velocity. Because of it, a change in the money supply will change aggregate spending and GNP by a predictable amount.

The chain of transmission from the money supply to GNP can be visualized as working roughly in the following fashion. Assume that the Federal Reserve increases the money supply through open-market purchases of government securities. This increases the liquidity of the public; they are now holding cash in place of government securities. However, people do not want simply to hold this additional money. According to the Monetarists, people want money mainly as a medium of exchange for day-to-day transactions purposes, or to hold for a short while before making purchases. Based on the current volume of transactions—represented by the current GNP—they already had just about the amount of money they needed. So, finding themselves with some extra money, they proceed to spend it on real assets, on real goods and services, thereby driving up GNP.

If the money supply was increased during a recession, then the increased spending primarily will raise employment and real output; on the other hand, if the economy was already close to full employment, then the increase in GNP will consist mainly of higher prices.

How high will GNP go? The answer, according to the Monetarists, is that spending on real goods and services will continue to climb until GNP has risen to the point where the relationship between it and the money supply becomes the same as it had been before the money supply was increased by the Federal Reserve. That relationship, of course, is exactly what we mean by monetary velocity (GNP/M). When GNP has reached the point where it once again stands in its previous ratio to the money supply, then the public will finally be satisfied to hold the increased stock of money as a medium of exchange and spending will level off.

The same thing could be said in still another way. The increase in the money supply makes the public's portfolio of assets more liquid than it had been. This increased liquidity leads to the purchase of additional (less liquid) real assets until the portfolio's liquidity is restored to its former state.

"Frank, how ever did you find this *guru?"*

Drawing by D. Fradon;
© 1968 The New Yorker Magazine, Inc.

A decrease in the money supply works in similar fashion, except in the opposite direction. When the Federal Reserve reduces the money supply through open market sales of government securities, the public finds itself short of cash relative to the volume of business being done. Spending on goods and services contracts, driving GNP lower until the previous relationship between GNP and the (now smaller) money supply is restored. Faced with a shortage of liquidity, the public cuts back its spending until GNP drops to the point where the original ratio of GNP to the money supply is reestablished and velocity falls back to "normal." GNP will then stabilize in line with the smaller money supply.

Now it is clear where the Monetarists got their name. We saw in the previous chapter that, from the point of view of the central bank, the ideal situation is where velocity is stable (or if it changes, that it does so gradually and predictably). This is precisely *the* main assumption of the Monetarists.

Given such conditions, the Federal Reserve can induce virtually any volume of spending it wants simply by adjusting the money supply to the known and dependable velocity. Monetary policy is both necessary *and sufficient* to control GNP. In the Monetarist World, there is no need to even pay any attention to fiscal policy (the Keynesians' pet). Changes in the money supply can do the whole job, and stabilization policy should concentrate on that and that alone. No wonder Monetarists blame the Federal Reserve whenever *anything* goes wrong!

The Keynesian View of Money

The gospel according to Saint John—the late John Maynard Keynes, that is—is that the channels through which the money supply affects GNP are rather different. They are less direct and also less reliable, primarily because velocity is not viewed as very stable in either the short or the long run.

The chain of transmission from the money supply to GNP can be visualized as follows. Assume once more that the Federal Reserve increases the money supply by open market purchases of government securities. Again, this increases the liquidity of the public. However, people *may* want simply to hold this additional liquidity. The entire process might end right there, before it has hardly begun. The public gets additional money and hoards it. Period. The money supply has increased but GNP is unaffected. Velocity has fallen. In the Keynesian World, unlike the Monetarist World, the public holds cash not only for day-to-day transactions purposes but *also* as idle balances or as a pool of liquidity for possible speculation in the stock and bond markets.

Suppose the Monetarists have a point: that people do *not* want to hold the additional cash. Finding themselves with more money, they proceed to spend it. In the Monetarist World they would spend it primarily on *real* assets, on real goods and services, thereby directly driving up GNP. In the Keynesian World, however, they would spend it not on real assets but on *financial* assets, such as stocks and bonds. The prices of securities rise and interest rates fall. The increased money supply may also increase the availability of credit as well as lower its cost. But GNP still has not been affected.

This drop in interest rates and increased availability of credit *may*, then, induce some business firms or consumers to borrow and purchase real goods and services. *Finally*, GNP has been affected.

A decrease in the money supply works in similar fashion. The Federal Reserve reduces the money supply so that the public finds itself short of cash. The public may just hold less cash and that will be that. GNP will not be affected. Or, in an effort to get more cash, the public may try to sell some *financial* assets (or buy less than it had been buying), driving securities prices down and interest rates up. The higher rates, and accompanying decreased availability of credit, *may* lead to less borrowing and less spending, finally reducing GNP.

To summarize the Keynesian view: a change in the money supply can only affect aggregate spending and GNP if it *first* changes interest rates and/or the availability of credit, and *then* only if business or consumer spending is sensitive to those changes. In this way of looking at things, there's many a possible slip 'twixt the cup and the lip.

Whither Goeth the Interest Rate?

It is obvious that to Keynesians one of the keys to the effectiveness of monetary policy is what happens to interest rates on financial instruments. Unless the increased liquidity produced by an expanding money supply lowers interest rates (and unless the decreased liquidity produced by contracting the money supply raises interest rates), monetary policy is probably impotent.

Even the wealth effect of monetary policy, mentioned near the end of Chapter 2, which has been invoked by latter-day Keynesians, operates through interest rates: higher interest rates imply lower securities prices, and lower interest rates imply higher securities prices. Such changes in wealth may or may not have a significant impact on spending. But if an expansionary monetary policy is to carry with it a wealth effect, it must lower interest rates; and if a contractionary monetary policy is to have a wealth effect, it must raise interest rates.

Monetarists, however, do not view interest rates as a major link in the transmission belt between a change in the money supply and the ultimate impact on spending. Indeed, in one version of Monetarism, if interest rates do not change at all it probably indicates a very *powerful* monetary policy, since presumably the entire change in liquidity is spent *directly* on goods and services and none at all in financial markets. Many Monetarists, however, argue that the impact of monetary policy on interest rates is often indeterminate: that an expansionary monetary policy often raises, instead of lowers, interest rates (and a contractionary policy often lowers them).

First of all, as noted, an increase in the money supply may be spent entirely on real assests; without spending on financial assets, interest rates will not fall. But even if the demand for financial assets does expand, driving interest rates down, the decline may be only temporary. If GNP goes up, interest rates will follow suit. As GNP rises, there is a greater need for day-to-day transactions cash to carry out the enlarging volume of business; firms will therefore borrow to raise more cash, and interest rates will rise.

Expectations are also invoked to demonstrate the indeterminacy of interest rates. For example, if an expansionary monetary policy generates inflationary expectations, interest rates will rise: lenders will not lend unless they obtain an interest rate sufficiently high to compensate them for receiving less valuable dollars when they are repaid their principal. If the going rate of interest is 3 percent, and an expansionary monetary policy generates expectations of 4 percent annual inflation, lenders will demand and borrowers will be willing to pay 7 percent. In terms of expected real purchasing power, the lender is receiving and the borrower is paying 3 percent—but nominal market rates will be 7 percent.

Can we really be this far in a book on monetary policy and say that we don't know which way interest rates respond to expansionary (or contractionary) monetary actions? Yes and no—unequivocally.

Monetarists and Keynesians generally agree that *initially* an expansionary policy lowers interest rates (and a contractionary policy raises them). But for how long? If the impact on real spending is strong, or if expectations of price changes are generated, the initial interest rate change will be reversed and rates may well snap back past what they had been originally. Thus interest rates could be either lower or higher at some point after an expansionary monetary policy, depending on the speed and strength of the response in GNP and on what happens to expectations regarding prices. (Similarly, interest rates could be either higher or lower at some point after tight money begins, depending on the same factors.)

The question of the strength of monetary policy in affecting GNP will be explored in detail in the following chapter. It should be obvious, however, that the Monetarist view implies a very direct and certain impact of money supply on economic activity. Money is only a temporary abode of purchasing power. Any increase in the money supply will soon be spent on goods and services. Thus Monetarists tend to believe that an expansionary monetary policy will be followed, rather shortly, by *higher* interest rates (and that a contractionary monetary policy will be followed by lower interest rates).

To Keynesians, the link between monetary policy and GNP is more tenuous. Changes in the money supply may or may not affect spending significantly. It depends partly on how much money the public wants to hold idle, and on the reaction of spending to changes in interest rates and credit availability. Most Keynesians—but by no means all —tend to believe that an expansionary monetary policy will be followed by *lower* interest rates for quite a while (and that a contractionary policy will be followed by higher interest for a considerable interval).

As an aside, we may note at this point that the Keynesians' skepticism regarding the efficacy of monetary policy is paralleled by their opposite stance on fiscal policy. Fiscal policy, you recall, is concerned with the manipulation of government expenditure and tax rates in order to influence economic activity. Keynesians believe that a change in government spending alters GNP directly; a change in tax rates alters consumer spending, also changing GNP. However, the Monetarists take issue with these alleged truths of Keynesian economics. We shall return to the details of fiscal policy and the arguments over its effectiveness in Chapter 12.

Is It Money or Credit?

A subsidiary but important debate between the Monetarists and the Keynesians is whether the Federal Reserve, in conducting monetary policy, should look only at the money supply or at overall credit conditions as well.

The Keynesian analysis is a *credit*, as opposed to a strictly *monetary*, chain of causation. In a sense, money per se is seen as not too important until it finds its way into the hands of a potential spender. To a Monetarist, anyone holding money is a likely spender. But to a Keynesian, a loan transaction may be necessary to move money from its current owner, who may be holding it idle, to a borrower who wants to spend it. Thus the Keynesians take a credit view, concerned with financial assets, credit availability, the direction of interest rates, the reaction of lenders and borrowers to rate changes, and the role of financial markets as conduits for funds.

To a Monetarist, all this is excess baggage, more harmful than helpful. It is money that counts, money per se, and its effects on GNP are not roundabout but direct. To look at anything else is only a distraction.

As an illustration of a case where the two views diverge, assume that funds move from an individual to a business firm in a loan transaction (say the purchase of a newly issued corporate bond). The money supply remains the same; the corporation now has more but the individual has less. To a Monetarist, there will be no net change in spending since there has been no change in the money supply; the business firm, with more money, will increase its spending; but this will be offset by the lender, with less money, decreasing his. A Keynesian, on the other hand, would say that the result is more likely to be a net increase in spending; the lender is probably parting with what were idle balances, which in the till of the borrowing corporation will now be activated. The money supply is unchanged, but its velocity will increase.

The Federal Reserve adheres essentially to a credit, rather than a strictly monetary, approach. Indeed, it frequently shies away from the term *monetary policy* in favor of the broader *monetary and credit policy*. Open market operations, reserve requirement changes, and discount rate movements affect credit conditions at least as much as they affect the money supply. Credit conditions include, among other things, interest rates on a wide variety of securities, the volume of activity in the various financial markets, bank reserve positions, credit extensions by commercial banks, and the flow of funds into and out of other financial institutions. The Federal Reserve considers all such credit conditions as well as the money supply when it decides what action it should or should not take.

In fact, for many years, the Federal Reserve's Board of Governors in Washington seemed to consider changes in the money supply only incidentally, perhaps not even on a par with other financial variables. Recently, however, prodded by the Monetarist-oriented Federal Reserve Bank of St. Louis, the money supply has become more prominent in board deliberations. Nevertheless, the skeptical attitude toward excessive emphasis on the money supply remains, as revealed by the label the board's research staff has pinned on the maverick St. Louis Bank's analytical framework—Brand X.

Who Is Right?

The Monetarists claim that monetary policy should be conducted only for the purpose of controlling the money supply. The Keynesians argue that interest rates and credit availability are even more significant. The Monetarists contend that changes in the money supply are the major reason for fluctuations in GNP. The Keynesians maintain that credit conditions are more important than the money supply, and, in any event, that fiscal policy is more important than either.

Ultimately, these differences can be settled only by empirical tests. As is often true in economic research, however, the factual evidence necessary to resolve the issues has been ambiguous at best and misleading at worst. There are credible (and incredible) empirical studies by eminent economists that come to diametrically opposite conclusions.

In the following chapter we will explore available evidence regarding the strength of monetary policy, and in Chapter 12 we will return to the debate. Although Monetarists and Keynesians may not be able to agree on theoretical issues, it is still possible that they might be able to reach a consensus in terms of policy. *If,* for example, most Keynesians were to conclude that a change in the money supply *does* change interest rates and/or the availability of credit in the direction they expect, and were to conclude further that spending on goods and services *is* sensitive to those changes, then they would see monetary policy as having a significant effect on GNP; the combatants might not be as far apart in practice as they are in theory.

PART II

The Power of the Purse

5

HOW EFFECTIVE IS

MONETARY POLICY?

If monetary policy is to alter GNP it cannot do it by mystic incantations. It has to do it by changing the consumer spending of households, the investment spending of business firms, or the expenditures of governments, either federal or state and local.

What categories of spending does monetary policy affect? To what extent? With what time lags? In contrast to the theoretical discussion in the previous chapter, and the velocity analysis of Chapter 3, the purpose of this chapter is to present the state of knowledge in this area as precisely—that is, in terms of numbers—as possible.

Time Lags in Monetary Policy

By their own admission, Federal Reserve officials are not omniscient. If the economy starts to slip into a recession, it takes time before the experts realize what is happening so they can take steps to correct it. Similarly, if inflation begins to accelerate, it takes a while before the evidence verifies the fact.

Prompt recognition of what the economy is doing is not as easy as it sounds. For one thing, the available data are often inadequate and frequently mixed: new car orders will rise while retail department store sales are falling; farm prices may be dropping while employment in urban areas is rising. Furthermore, the economy rarely proceeds on a perfectly smooth course, either up or down. Every upsweep is interrupted from time to time by erratic dips; every decline into recession is punctuated irregularly by false signs of progress, which then evaporate. Is a change only a brief and temporary interruption of an already existing trend, or is it the start of a new trend in the opposite direction? No one is ever perfectly sure. This problem of getting an accurate "fix" on what is happening in the economy, or what is likely to happen in the near future, is called the *recognition lag* in monetary policy. In 1968–69, for example, the Federal Reserve did not recognize that inflation was as serious a problem as it turned out to be until rising prices had gathered too much momentum to be halted.

As soon as the recognition lag ends, the *impact lag* begins, spanning the time from when the central bank starts using one of its tools, say open market operations, until an effect is evident on the ultimate objective—aggregate spending in the economy. It may take weeks before interest rates change significantly after a monetary action has begun. Changes in credit availability and money supply also take time. And a further delay is probable before actual spending decisions are affected. Once monetary policy does start to influence spending, however, it will most likely continue to have an impact on GNP for quite a while.

Regarding the recognition lag, rough evidence suggests that the Federal Reserve generally starts to ease about half a year or more after a boom has already run its course, whereas it starts to tighten only about three months after the trough in a business cycle. This evidence is less than definitive, and it is likely that under some circumstances the monetary authorities will sense what is going on and take action more promptly than under other circumstances. Nevertheless, the inference that the central bank is typically more concerned with preventing inflation than with avoiding recession probably contains a grain of truth.

The impact lag is most conveniently discussed, along with the strength of monetary policy, in terms of the results that formal econometric models of the economy have produced. An econometric model is a mathematical-statistical representation that describes how the economy behaves. Such a model gives empirical content to theoretical propositions about how individuals and business firms, lenders and borrowers, savers and spenders react to economic stimuli. After such relationships are formalized in a mathematical expression, data on past experience in the real world are used to estimate the precise behavioral pattern of each sector. A model, therefore, is based on real-world observations jelled into a formal pattern by the grace of statistical techniques. Thrown into a computer, the model simulates the economy in action and grinds out predictions based on the formal interactions the model embodies.

Our knowledge of how best to construct such a model is still fairly rudimentary. The same data can produce different results depending on the theoretical propositions used to construct the model. As one cynic put it, "If one tortures the data long enough, it will confess."

A Keynesian model, for instance, would incorporate different behavioral assumptions than a Monetarist model and hence grind out an alternative set of predictions. Furthermore, the data we have available to feed in are not all that we would like. In any case, past relationships are not always reliable guides to future behavior; if they were, the favorite would always win the football game and marriages would never end in divorce.

Nevertheless, despite all their shortcomings, such models, if carefully and objectively constructed, are probably superior to casual off-the-cuff observations followed by inadequately supported generalizations. They are superior, that is, provided they are always taken with a healthy dose of skepticism.

The Federal Reserve board, together with economists at the Massachusetts Institute of Technology and the University of Pennsylvania, have developed an econometric model of the behavior of economic aggregates in the United States. Many other economists have done similar work at other universities and financial institutions. But our discussion will be based primarily on the Federal Reserve–MIT–Penn model, affectionately called the FMP model, which was prepared specifically to evaluate the impact of stabilization policies on economic activity. The results of Monetarist models, such as the one constructed at the Federal Reserve Bank of St. Louis, will be contrasted with the FMP model.

The Impact of Monetary Policy on GNP

The latest edition of the FMP model—and there have been numerous editions—includes virtually every conceivable linkage (maybe) between monetary policy and real economic activity. Interest rate effects, wealth effects, and credit availability are all explicitly articulated in mathematical splendor. As a first approximation to measuring the

"The machine then selects the likely equations from a complicated pattern of theoretical probables. It calculates these, and the correct answer is printed on a card. Then our Miss Swenson files them God knows where, and we can never find the damn things again."

Drawing by Chon Day
© 1971 The New Yorker Magazine, Inc.

impact of monetary policy, let us look at what the model says about the effect of changes in the money supply on spending (i.e., on GNP). An increase in the money supply of $1 billion produces an increase of $1.5 billion in GNP after six months. At the end of one year GNP rises by $2.5 billion, and at the end of two years it is nearly $6 billion above its initial level. After three years, economic activity is still rising, producing an increase of more than $10 billion in GNP above its original level.

These results imply a rather long lag before the full effects of an increase in the money supply are felt on spending. If the Federal Reserve undertakes an expansionary monetary policy now, it will have to contend with the effects of such policies well into the future. This can create serious problems for monetary policy, as we shall later see.

Monetarists, especially those of the St. Louis variety, are unhappy with the FMP model. They don't like the detailed description of the transmission mechanism between money and economic activity, suspecting that the architects of the model may have unwittingly left out some of the *direct* links between money and spending. Exactly what these links are is not for us to know—but money works in mysterious ways, so we must have faith. The Federal Reserve Bank of St. Louis pits the midwestern virtue of simplicity against the sophisticated system produced by the Boston-Philadelphia-Washington Establishment.

The simple St. Louis model relating GNP directly to money produces a much faster and initially larger impact of money on economic activity. According to the St. Louis model, an increase of $1 billion in the money supply raises GNP by over $3 billion after six months and by over $5 billion after one year, roughly double the impact derived from the FMP model after the same time intervals. After one year, however, the St. Louis model finds no additional impact of money on GNP.

The FMP economists counter that the little black box connecting money and GNP in the St. Louis model does not lend itself to scientific evaluation. It is impossible to tell how much of the change in GNP is really due to changes in money supply and how much is due to other things that are changing at the same time. In short, the St. Louis model is too simple to be trusted by Easterners.

Some economists have argued that the effectiveness of monetary policy is asymmetrical—that is, monetary policy is more effective in stopping inflation than in getting us out of recession. They reason that the high interest rates and curtailed availability of credit that characterize tight money cannot help but force restrictions on spending, while the low interest rates and ample credit availability that are typical of easy money will not necessarily induce people to borrow and spend. You can lead a horse to water, as the saying goes, but you can't make him drink.

The FMP model provides some support for an asymmetrical response to tight versus easy money. In particular, a *decrease* of $1 billion in the money supply lowers GNP by $4 billion after one year and by $8 billion after two years. Thus the impact of tight money is more than one-third larger than the impact of easy money. The St. Louis model, however, makes no distinction between periods of easy or tight money. According to the Monetarists, money is money and if you want it and don't have it, it is equally as disturbing as when you have it and don't want it. (Yes, the sentence is written correctly; we checked it three times and so did the proofreaders.)

Returning to the question of time lags, it should be noted that it takes time for an open market operation by the Federal Reserve to have an impact on the money supply.

Reserves provided through open market purchases, for example, must work their way through the banking system as banks make loans and buy securities. If we take as the starting point for monetary policy an injection of about $300 million worth of reserves via an open market purchase, this raises the money supply by about $1 billion after six to nine months. GNP, meanwhile, increases by a little less than $1 billion after six months, by about $2 billion after one year, as compared with our previous figure of $2.5 billion. If we measure the lag in monetary policy from the point in time when the Federal Reserve injects reserves through open market operations, the total lag becomes somewhat longer than was suggested in the first two paragraphs of this section.

The Effect of Monetary Policy on Interest Rates

The impact of monetary policy on interest rates is also generated by our econometric models. Here again Monetarist models differ somewhat from the Keynesian variety. *All* models show that interest rates decline and remain below their original levels for at least six months to a year after an expansionary monetary policy and that they are above their original levels after a contractionary monetary policy for a similar period. The FMP model, for example, shows that a $1 billion increase in reserves via open market purchases by the Federal Reserve lowers the corporate bond rate by one-fourth of 1 percentage point initially; after some slight readjustment upward during the next twelve months, it levels off and remains below its original level for a considerable length of time.

The more sensitive three-month Treasury bill rate reacts with greater gyrations to an open market purchase. Immediately following a $1 billion purchase of government securities by the Federal Reserve, the bill rate declines by more than 1 percentage point. But after one year the bill rate is only one-half of 1 percentage point below its original level, and it eventually comes to rest about one-third of 1 percentage point below its starting point. Under certain conditions, the FMP model does suggest that interest rates could rise above their original levels in response to an expansionary monetary policy: namely, when inflationary price expectations are especially strong. Even here, however, the decline in rates lasts at least through the second year of expansion. In contrast, there are some Monetarist models that show the Treasury bill rate snapping back to its original level and going above within six to twelve months after an expansionary monetary policy.

Thus far we have discussed the overall impact of monetary policy on GNP, but we have not explored the particular categories of spending involved. Monetary policy does not have an equal impact on all types of expenditure. Which kinds of spending does it affect most, and which kinds of spending appear to be relatively immune?

Investment Spending

One would expect that interest rates and investment spending should move in opposite directions: that an increase in interest rates, for example, should lower investment spending. If the cost of borrowing rises, business firms should presumably be less willing to incur new debt in order to build new factories or buy new equipment. The historical record shows, however, that interest rates and business investment almost always move in the *same* direction. As in most cases where fact contradicts economic theory, one of them must give ground—and it is usually fact.

In the historical record, many things are happening simultaneously, so that separate strands of cause and effect are not sorted out. Investment spending is influenced by a number of factors besides interest rates—by sales expectations, changes in anticipated profitability, pressures from competitors who may be installing new equipment, the degree of capacity currently being utilized, the availability of internal funds (undivided profits and depreciation reserves), expectations regarding labor costs, and expectations regarding inflation, to name only some. An increase in interest rates may inhibit investment, and yet investment may, in fact, rise if a number of these other elements shift sufficiently to offset the effect of a rise in interest costs.

The actual change in investment spending from one year to the next reflects the net impact of *all* the variables influencing it, not just interest rates alone. We would expect, however, that if interest rates had not risen, investment would probably have expanded even further.

Econometric methods permit isolation of specific factors, allowing us to experiment in the "laboratory" of statistical techniques, as it were. The effects of interest rates on investment, for example, can be examined holding all other influences constant. The results show that a rise in interest rates does reduce investment spending. In the Federal Reserve's model, for example, an increase of one percentage point (say, from 7 to 8 percent) in the corporate bond rate lowers business spending on new plant and equipment by about half a billion dollars after one year, by about $2.5 billion after two years, and by $4 billion after three years.

In this instance, the time lag is clearly quite substantial. In most cases, investment decisions are not made in the morning and executed in the afternoon. Decisions regarding the installation of new machinery and the construction of new plants are usually made many months in advance of their actual execution. Thus an increase in rates does not promptly affect investment spending. What it does affect is *decisions* currently being made about plans that will not actually be *implemented* until months or years in the future.

The FMP model does reveal, however, that there is one category of investment spending that is extremely sensitive to a change in interest rates. That category is residential construction, which, although it is not business investment, is still generally considered a form of investment because of the long time horizon involved, with returns accruing for many years into the future. An increase of one percentage point in the interest rate lowers housing expenditures by $2 billion within nine months and by $3 billion after a year. In addition to this interest rate effect, residential construction is also affected by monetary policy through credit rationing by financial institutions engaged in mortgage lending. Some of the implications of this strong relationship between monetary policy and home-building are explored further in Chapter 18.

Small business perhaps deserves special mention in any discussion of the impact of monetary policy on investment expenditures. Spokesmen for small business have always contended that during periods of tight money, commercial banks discriminate against them in their allocation of scarce loanable funds.

The evidence on this is not altogether clear, but it is likely that small firms are indeed at a disadvantage relative to large borrowers during periods when banks are short of funds. Furthermore, large firms have access to the corporate bond market, the commercial paper market, and other alternative sources of funds, while small firms do not.

On the other hand, the extension of trade credit (delayed payment for supplies) from large to small firms tends to offset some of these disadvantages. In effect, through their supplier-customer relationships, the large firms pass their access to funds on to the smaller firms in the form of trade credit. To some extent this alleviates the problem, although it is not likely that it eliminates it.

State and Local Government Spending and Consumer Spending

Construction expenditures by state and local governments also appear sensitive to the actions of the monetary authorities. Municipal bond flotations are often reduced, postponed, or completely canceled during periods of high and rising interest rates. Many municipal governments have self-imposed interest rate ceilings that eliminate them from the market when rates go up. In other instances, when interest costs become too heavy, local voters become reluctant to approve bond issues for school construction and other projects, since the higher interest burden implies the immediate or eventual imposition of higher property or sales taxes.

The FMP model indicates that a one percentage point rise in the interest rate cuts state and local government spending by almost $2 billion after six months. Subsequently, however, the impact declines as the municipalities rethink their problems and, typically, proceed sooner or later with much of their planned expenditures.

Consumer spending, according to the FMP model, is affected by monetary policy directly through the wealth effect of monetary actions on the values of stocks and bonds in household portfolios, and indirectly through the impact on the level of income. About one-third of the impact of monetary policy on GNP after one year occurs through changes in consumer spending, with another third coming from residential construction and the remainder divided between plant and equipment spending by businesses and spending by state and local governments. The effects on consumer spending continue to build up during the second and third years following a monetary action, while the impact on housing tends to stabilize as credit rationing by financial institutions becomes less important. After the first year, the thrust of monetary policy is reinforced by the delayed effects on business plant and equipment spending.

Lags Again

The evidence presented by both Monetarists and Keynesians suggests that monetary policy does have a significant impact on economic activity, with much of the impact distributed over two calendar years. There are powerful short-run effects but, at least as far as the FMP model is concerned, even more powerful long-run effects.

When the initial *recognition lag* is combined with the *impact lags*, however, the usefulness of monetary policy as a stabilization device becomes less obvious. Suppose a boom tops out in January but the Federal Reserve does not realize it is over until July, at which time monetary policy starts to ease. Its pre-July tightness may still be having depressing effects through the first half of the *following year*, but by then we might well be in the middle of a recession and in need of exactly the opposite medicine. The Federal Reserve, of course, will be providing that opposite medicine, but its expansionary effects may be so long delayed that they might not take hold until we are in another boom, thus once again making matters worse. Monetary policy will be a destabilizer rather than a stabilizer!

We shall return to the crucial topic of time lags in Chapter 11, where we discuss the optimum execution of monetary policy.

6

IS MONEY THE INFLATION

CULPRIT?

Arthur F. Burns, appointed by President Nixon to the post of Chairman of the Board of Governors of the Federal Reserve System, told a visitor, "One of the greatest evils of inflation is that it leaves the president with no easy choices." When asked whether he thought the voters appreciate a real effort to stop inflation, he responded, "I like to think you are rewarded at the polls. But even if the reward isn't at the polls, I come from a culture where there is a belief in a reward in the hereafter."

Those of you who have been valiantly searching for the Eleventh Commandment can now rest easy; "Thou shalt fight inflation" has just been added to the scriptures!

To most of us, inflation is not something we pray for or against in houses of worship, but something we encounter in supermarkets, department stores, and, of course, doctors' offices. Needless to say, prices today are quite different even from what they were only twenty-five years ago. Workers and businessmen whose incomes have risen along with the rising prices of the past quarter century can still visit their favorite stores and hospitals, although they probably can't stay as long as they used to in either place. But inflation is a more painful matter for many others, especially for the elderly and for retired or disabled people whose incomes are more or less fixed for the rest of their lives. At a sustained annual increased of 3 percent, prices will double every twenty-four years; at an increase of 4 percent, they will double every seventeen and a half years; and if prices were to go up at the rate of 5 percent annually, they would double every fourteen years.

Under such circumstances, it is obvious that retirement incomes of a fixed dollar amount gradually melt away. A retirement income that is initially adequate slowly becomes marginal, and, as the years continue to unfold, it approaches the level of sheer subsistence. About the only thing many older people can hope for is that they reach the hereafter before inflation does.

Who is responsible for inflation? Is money the culprit? Can we bring an inflationary spiral to a halt if we clamp down on the money supply? Can wage-price controls help?

Too Much Money Chasing Too Few Goods

The classic explanation of inflation is that "too much money is chasing too few goods." The diagnosis implies the remedy; stop creating so much money and inflation will disappear.

Such a diagnosis has indeed been accurate, painfully so, during those hard-to-believe episodes in history when runaway inflation skyrocketed prices out of sight and plunged the value of money to practically zero. Example: prices quadrupled in revolutionary America between 1775 and 1780, when the Continental Congress opened the printing presses and flooded the country with currency. The phrase "not worth a continental" remains to this day. Germany after World War I was even more extreme; prices in 1923 were 34 billion times what they had been in 1921. In Hungary during World War II it took 1.4 nonillion pengoes in 1946 to buy what one pengo could purchase a few years earlier (one nonillion equals 1,000,000,000,000, 000,000,000,000,000,000).

Pathological breakdowns of this sort are impossible unless they are fueled by continuous injections of new money in ever-increasing volume. In such cases, money is undoubtedly the inflation culprit, and the one and only way to stop the avalanche from gathering momentum is to slam a quick brake on the process of money creation.

Creeping Inflation

However, hyperinflation is not what we have been experiencing in this country in recent years. During World War II, consumer prices rose by about 20 percent. In the immediate postwar years (1945–49), after wage and price controls were removed, they climbed another 35 percent. None of this was unexpected or particularly unusual. Prices typically rise in wartime and immediately thereafter.

The unusual thing about prices during World War II and its aftermath is not that they rose so much during and immediately after it. What *is* unusual is that they have never declined since. Quite the contrary, prices have continued onward and upward to this day, virtually without interruption, producing the longest period of continuous inflation in American history. In all prior wars, prices had gone up during and immediately after hostilities, but then had fallen back somewhat. Not this time. In all prior peacetimes, price increases had been interrupted from time to time by occasional corrective periods of stable or declining prices. No longer.

From 1949 through 1972, the cost of living increased in every year but one (1955). The annual rate of inflation over the entire period averages out at over 2 percent per year. Its persistence, month after month, year after year, has resulted in an aggregate 70 percent increase in the cost of living.

This is not hyperinflation. It is not like America in 1775, Germany in 1923, or Hungary in 1946. This is a different sort of animal—nibbling away doggedly, insistently, without pause, at the purchasing power of the dollar. Prices do not skyrocket, they only creep—some years 2 percent, some years 3 or 4 percent—but always in one direction, always up, up, up.

This type of inflation is something new. Is money the culprit here, too? Can creeping inflation, like hyperinflation, be stopped simply by slamming the brakes on the money supply? To work our way around these questions, it will be helpful to examine the recent inflation process a bit more closely.

Demand Pull

We understand fairly clearly—as well as anything is understood in economics, anyway—why the price level rises when aggregate demand exceeds the limits of the economy's full capacity output. This is the orthodox inflation setting, exemplified in starkest form in wartime when we simply cannot produce enough goods and services to satisfy all would-be purchasers at existing prices. The excessive spending (in relation to the available supply) bids prices up, thereby eliminating some potential buyers and, in effect, rationing the available short supply among those able and willing to pay more.

War generates the classic form of demand-pull inflation, with competition among buyers for the available goods and services driving prices higher. Men are put to work producing war goods—which are bought by the government—but the incomes they receive, unless siphoned off by higher taxes, are as available as ever for the purchase of private consumer goods and services. At the same time, the output of civilian goods is curtailed as war production takes precedence.

Part of the reason for our inability to eliminate the inching up of prices is simply that we have never really brought World War II to a complete end. An entire generation has grown up that has never fully known peace. Intermittently, in the past two decades, the financial, manpower, and matériel resources of the nation have been mobilized in an effort to produce both guns *and* butter. Budget deficits, shortages, and accelerated consumer and business buying plans have periodically converged, with the swollen aggregate demand outpacing the economy's productive capacity.

Cost Push

But that cannot be the whole story. For there have been periods of relative tranquillity, primarily in the late 1950s and early 1960s, when international tensions eased and slack developed in the economy. But even then prices continued upward, although at a somewhat more leisurely pace. For example, aggregate demand from government, business, and consumers was in no sense excessive during the years 1958 through 1964. If anything, it was rather sluggish. Unemployment averaged close to 6 percent of the civilian labor force during that seven-year period, and frequently exceeded 7 percent during two of the years (1958 and 1961). Nevertheless, prices inched up year after year, including those years—1958 and 1961—when unemployment and idle capacity were particularly evident. By the end of 1964, consumer prices were 10 percent higher than they had been at the end of 1957.

Why should prices rise, as they did from 1957 through 1964, when spending is slow and we are far below full employment of our labor force and full capacity utilization of our industrial plant? In past years, before World War II, these were the very times when prices *fell* and the impact of prior inflation was to some extent ameliorated. Some new ingredients have evidently entered the picture since the 1930s, and drastically altered the economy's response mechanism.

One such ingredient is the economic strength of labor unions. The American Federation of Labor was founded in 1886, but the real power of trade unions to influence money-wages came with the passage of the Wagner Act and related legislation half a century later. On the basis of government encouragement of unionism as a declared principle of public policy, the expansion of the economy from the depression of the 1930s into the war boom of the 1940s carried with it an enormous growth in union membership. The ranks of organized labor jumped from 3 million members in 1933 to 9 million in 1940 and to 15 million in 1946. Today, union rolls list about 20 million members. The Taft-Hartley Act of 1947 corrected some union abuses, but it put hardly a dent in their new-found power to extract wage increases in excess of productivity growth, thereby generating round after round of higher production costs.

The second new ingredient—closely related to the economic power of organized labor, although not so recent an arrival—is the substantial market power of big business. Because of the nature of modern technology, which often results in lower unit production costs as the scale of operations expands, a few large firms dominate many major manufacturing industries. Their size enables these industrial giants to exert a degree of control over their prices that would be impossible in a thoroughgoing competitive environment, thereby permitting them, to some extent, to pass cost increases on to their customers.

The third new ingredient is the Employment Act of 1946, under which the government assumed responsibility for maintaining full employment through the use of its monetary, fiscal, and related powers. According to the Employment Act, "it is the continuing policy and responsibility of the federal government to use all practicable means . . . to promote maximum employment, production, and purchasing power."

Without the support of the Employment Act, neither Big Labor nor Big Business, individually or in concert, could sustain a wage-price spiral for very long. In the absence of the Employment Act, labor would have to take more seriously the possibility that it might be jacking up money-wages too far, that excessive wage demands might force businessmen to cut back on their hiring. Businessmen would similarly have to guard against pricing themselves out of the market. But such restraints are relaxed by the presence of a full employment guarantee underwritten by

Big Government, standing by to "insure prosperity" with injections of purchasing power should employment or sales decline too far.

The old-fashioned pattern of demand-pull inflation— excess aggregate spending, greater than the economy's productive capacity, pulling prices up—has not disappeared. Witness the Korean War period, the 1956–57 episode, and Vietnam. But demand-pull (or buyers') inflation has been joined in the postwar period by a new form of inflation— cost-push (or sellers') inflation. Even when aggregate spending subsides, as from 1958 through 1964, prices still rise. The distinguishing feature of cost-push or sellers' inflation is a rising price level while the economy is still well below a full employment (full capacity) rate of production.

Even when full employment is far distant on the horizon, Big Labor and Big Business start to turn the screws. Backed by substantial market (and political) power of their own, underwritten by a full employment guarantee that gives immunity—at least to some extent—from the consequences of their actions, strong unions and large corporations begin throwing their weight around and marking wages and prices up even when aggregate demand is weak and anemic. As we move closer and closer to full employment, they gradually become more aggressive until, in the immediate neighborhood of full employment, the pressure for higher wages and prices becomes literally explosive. At this point, for all practical purposes, cost and demand become virtually indistinguishable as they interact, reinforcing each other.

Indeed, it is somewhat artificial to separate the two kinds of inflation to begin with; wage increases in excess of productivity growth mean higher costs for the businessman, thereby putting upward cost pressure on prices. Those same higher wages also mean larger incomes for wage-earners, thereby generating a step-up in consumer spending that yanks prices up from the demand side. The stage is then set for a new round of wage negotiations based on the increase in the cost of living, as the process feeds on itself and continues ad infinitum, or is it ad nauseam?

Money and Creeping Inflation

Unlike hyperinflation, money is not so clearly and uniquely the culprit when it comes to the real problem of our times, creeping inflation. The "fit" between the money supply and the cost of living exists, but it is rather loose and a bit baggy. Like a 36C liberated woman, things tend to jiggle around quite a bit.

Take, for example, the last four decades:

1. From the end of 1930 to the end of 1940, the money supply increased by 70 percent, but prices, instead of rising, fell 15 percent.

2. From 1940 to 1950, the money supply increased by 175 percent, but prices rose by only 80 percent, less than half as much.

3. From the end of 1950 to the end of 1960 provides the best fit; the money supply grew by about 25 percent and the consumer price index rose by about 20 percent.

4. However, from 1960 through 1970 the relationship sags again; the money supply increased by 40 percent, but prices by just 20 percent.

Even the close relationship during the 1950s turns out to be less impressive upon further examination. During the first half of the decade the money supply increased twice as fast as prices, while during the second half prices increased twice as rapidly as the money supply. At the end of the 1960s, the money supply was about 4½ times larger than it had been in 1940, but prices were "only" about 2½ times higher.

This is not meant to imply that money has nothing to do with creeping inflation. Quite the contrary, it has a great deal to do with it indeed, if only because, sooner or later, people simply will not be able to continue buying the same amount of goods and services at higher and higher prices unless the money supply increases. If the money supply today were no larger than it was in 1940 ($40 billion), or even than it was in 1950 ($115 billion), prices would have stopped rising long ago. Over the long run, an increase in the money supply is a *necessary* condition for the continuation of inflation, creeping or otherwise.

But it is not a *sufficient* condition. Increases in the money supply do not always result in inflation. An increase in the money supply will not raise prices if velocity falls (as in the 1930s). Even if velocity remains constant, an increase in the money supply will not raise prices if production expands. When we are in a depression, for example, the spending stimulated by an increase in the money supply is likely to raise output and employment rather than prices. Furthermore, in the short run at least, and sometimes the short run is a matter of several years, increased spending and inflation can be brought about by increases in velocity without any increase in the money supply, as we saw in Chapter 3.

Nevertheless, it bears repeating that inflation can only persist for any length of time by grace of the central bank. If the inflation is primarily demand-pull, a cutback—or merely stability—in the money supply will sooner or later put an end to further increases in spending and thereby eliminate, or at least substantially moderate, the upward drift of prices. If the inflation is primarily cost-push, a cutback or stability in the money supply will sooner or later make it difficult, if not impossible, for business firms to sell their products at higher and higher prices—and thereby make it equally impossible for them to continue granting wage increases in excess of productivity growth, no matter how strong labor may be.

Let us end this section with a summary statement of the role of money with respect to inflation. Does more money always lead to inflation? No, but it can, under certain circumstances, and if the increase is large enough it probably will. Case 1: If the central bank expands the money supply while we are in a recession, then the increased spending it induces is likely to lead to more employment and a larger output of goods and services rather than to higher prices. Case 2: As we approach full employment and capacity output, increases in the money supply become more and more likely to generate rising prices. However, if this increase is only large enough to provide funds for the enlarged volume of transactions accompanying real economic growth, inflation still need not result. Case 3: Thus only when the money supply increases under conditions of high employment *and* exceeds the requirements of economic growth can it be held responsible for kindling an inflationary spiral.

The time horizon and the extent of inflation are also relevant. In the short run, an increase in monetary velocity alone, with a constant or even declining money supply, can finance a modest volume of inflationary spending. The longer the time span, however, and the higher prices rise, the less likely that velocity can do the job by itself. Over the longer run, the money supply must expand for inflation to persist.

Conclusions: more money does not always lead to inflation (Cases 1 and 2), but sometimes it does (Case 3). In
the short run, inflation can make some headway without
any change in the money supply, but rising prices cannot
proceed too far too long without the sanction of the central
bank.

The Trade-off between Price Stability
and Employment

Since inflation is not something we want any more of, and
since the tools to curb it are at hand, why don't we just
use them and put a stop to these never-ending increases in
the cost of living?

The reason we hesitate is because of an apparent conflict of national objectives. The cost of price stability—in
terms of the unemployment necessary to get it—is too high.
If we pursued monetary (and fiscal) policies with the
determination necessary to put a total and complete brake
on inflation, we would probably find outselves with unemployment of at least 8 percent of the labor force. We do not
want any more inflation, but we do not want any more
depressions either. And so far we have been unable to find
a solution to the problem of stopping rising prices without
simultaneously bringing on at least a recession.

To put the problem succinctly, it seems that we cannot
have both price stability and full employment at one and
the same time. If we want stable prices, we have to sacri-
fice full employment. And if we want a high level of employment, we have to give up stable prices. Exactly what
are the terms of this trade-off?

On the basis of our experience during the 1960s, the accompanying illustration—known as a Phillips Curve, after its popularizer, Professor A. W. Phillips—gives a rough idea of the cost, in terms of unemployment, of various degrees of price stability. For example, point A (1.2 percent inflation, 5.7 percent unemployment) represents the situation in 1963; point B (4 percent inflation, 3.5 percent unemployment) represents 1968.

As the Phillips Curve indicates, obtaining absolute price stability during the 1960s would have required an estimated 8 percent unemployment rate, a rather high cost indeed. But reaching full employment (defined as consistent with 3.5 or 4 percent unemployment, on the grounds that most of those workers in the 3.5 or 4 percent category were voluntarily between jobs or preferred fishing to working) would have resulted in an inflation rate close to 4 percent a year, also no small price to pay.

Furthermore (and this the chart does not indicate), for well over a decade the black unemployment rate has been

Prices and Employment: The Trade-off

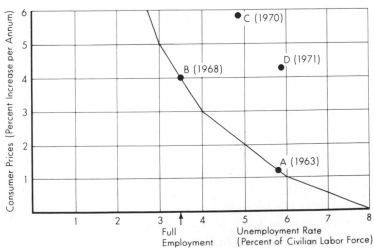

approximately twice the national average. An overall national unemployment rate of 8 percent, which is about what it would have taken to elimate inflation completely during the 1960s, implies a black unemployment rate at the deep depression level of 16 percent. Even worse, the black teen-age unemployment rate has been averaging *seven* times the overall jobless rate for many years; an overall national unemployment rate of 8 percent means a black teen-age unemployment rate of more than 50 percent.

The optimum choice among this array of less-than-happy alternatives is not amenable to a purely economic solution. If we choose high employment (say no more than 3.5 percent unemployment), then some people will be hurt by the substantial inflation. On the other hand, if we move toward the lower part of the curve and choose something close to stable prices, then other people will be hurt by the heavy unemployment. An economist, as an economist, has no basis on which he can judge whether it is better to help Peter and hurt Paul, or to help Paul and hurt Peter. The resolution of this conflict of interests fundamentally involves personal value judgments and assessments of the social implications of the alternatives more than it involves economics.

But things are even more complicated. Historical relationships are subject to change. In the early 1970s, a bad situation has gotten even worse, as points C and D on the diagram indicate. Today, a policy-maker who looks at the 1960s' Phillips Curve and chooses full employment, expecting that it will be accompanied by 4 percent inflation, will wind up generating a considerably higher rate of inflation than 4 percent. And if he reaches for absolute price stability, judging from points C and D he will get not 8 percent unemployment but lots more to boot.

What happened? Where has the Phillips Curve gone? To the right—along with other elder statesmen—is the simplest answer, and the one that appeals to most Keynesians. The trade-off between stable prices and full employment has simply gotten worse. A changed composition of the labor force, an expansion in the demand for skilled labor but not for unskilled, more aggressive union behavior, increased market power in the hands of the large corporations, and other factors have all pushed the Phillips Curve to the right.

The Monetarist Challenge
to the Phillips Curve

And yet there is a still more mind-boggling possibility—no Phillips Curve at all. The trade-off between stable prices and high employment is illusory. That towering iconoclast, Milton Friedman, has pounced upon another victim!

The Monetarist reasoning goes something like this. Government policies to increase employment generate rising prices; some additional employment can initially be bought with higher prices. But workers are not fools. They soon realize that rising prices are eroding the value of their pay raises. If they were satisfied with 3 percent pay raises before, now they will want more to keep pace with inflation. If we assume 4 percent inflation has been generated, for example, workers will want 7 percent pay raises now in order to get a 3 percent *real* wage increase. If employers believe they can pass on such a wage increase in the form of higher prices, they will grant it—thereby making the inflation worse. Then, as the day follows the night, the unions will want even larger money-wage increases if they are to wind up with a 3 percent real wage hike. Thus expectations of further inflation snowball through round after round of ever-growing wage settlements promptly followed by corresponding price increases. Right on!

On such grounds, Friedman argues that there is no true trade-off between employment and prices, because in the long run you can't fool all of the people very much of the time. You may be able to buy some additional employment with higher prices for a while, but as soon as workers catch on that their pay raises are more imaginary than real either the inflation will accelerate or businessmen will begin to lay off workers. In either case, the Phillips Curve doesn't give the correct answer to the question of how high prices would rise if employment were increased by a given amount.

What should be done?

Nothing—says Friedman. Let the economy find its own natural level of unemployment. Don't try to lower unemployment by inflating. It will only help for a short while, and the more you do it the less you get!

Is all this true? To some extent, yes. In the long run, the trade-off between employment and prices does get worse, as the chart indicates. But all evidence points to a rather long run—say ten or fifteen years—before all the employment effects of increased inflation are wiped out. We can still use inflation to buy some employment—but less than we thought and for a shorter time period.

Wage-Price Controls and All That

There are other means that have been proposed—and even implemented—to help resolve the inflation-unemployment quandry. These include manpower training programs, index-linked bonds, escalating annuities and social security payments, and—for those of you who haven't heard —wage-price controls.

Manpower programs are aimed at shifting the dismal Phillips Curve to the left. There is substantial agreement that the fundamental cause of the present position of the Phillips Curve is the failure of labor markets to operate effectively. Less inflation would be associated with any given level of aggregate demand and employment if workers who are between jobs could be placed more quickly, if disadvantaged workers who make up the "hard core unemployed" could be retrained with skills that are in short supply, and if artificial barriers to entry were removed from certain trades and occupations. Manpower programs designed to rectify some or all of these inefficiencies in the way our economy utilizes its labor force might very well permit us to coexist with an unfriendly Phillips Curve by pushing it to the left.

Since the basic problem with inflation is that it imposes costs—in the form of erosion of purchasing power—on certain segments of the public (widows living on pensions, and others whose income is more or less fixed in dollar terms), it is conceivable that one way to get around the problem of inflation is to compensate those who suffer most. This could be achieved by linking annuities and social security payments to some cost-of-living index. This has been billed as "living with inflation" by James Tobin of Yale and Leonard Ross of Columbia. The main drawback of such arrangements is that they may lull us into complacency about inflation—"try it, you'll like it"—and increase the likelihood of hyperinflation.

Which brings us to the "most impractical, least likely to be implemented anti-inflationary scheme of all"—wage-price controls. (Wha?) There are many types of wage-price policies—the strong variety, best approximated by wartime controls with stiff legal sanctions and rationing, and the weak variety, consisting of appeals to labor and business to act with restraint and integrity. Well, as the poet said, "integrity ain't all that it's cracked up to be"—so much for the effectiveness of the weak form of wage-price controls. As for the strong form of controls—few would argue, save perhaps John Kenneth Galbraith, that the benefits flowing from a full-blown set of wage-price controls would even remotely justify the bureaucratic costs and inefficiencies typically incurred in their implementation. This leaves us with the middle ground—temporary wage-price freezes and wage-price controls with gum disease (that is, lacking teeth).

Wage-price controls once again involve trying to shift the Phillips Curve to the left. This time, however, we merely try to supress some of the inflation associated with a given level of employment. But the costs cannot really be escaped. Inflation is inequitable—to those living on relatively fixed incomes; but so are wage-price controls—to those who were slow in joining the inflationary wage-price spiral before the controls were imposed. Even more serious is the interference of wage-price controls with the price mechanism that is so vital in channeling resources to where they are most desired in a decentralized unplanned economy. If people want more sex, they bid up the price and resources flow in that direction. Even Professor Galbraith must admit that this is a good thing. Indeed, even centrally planned economies appear to be moving toward *greater* reliance on decentralized price-profit signals to direct resources to their best uses.

Many European countries that have experimented with rather permanent wage-price controls (called incomes policies across the Atlantic) have concluded that they don't really work. Methods of getting around controls are developed as time passes—making them both ineffective and more inequitable. As an interim measure, however, wage-price controls may have a greater justification and a better track record. If conditions are ripe for a slowdown in inflation (6 percent unemployment?), but inflationary expectations have become a way of life, the imposition of controls may have some shock value. By most standards, the three-month wage-price freeze of 1971 was a success, probably because of this reason. Furthermore, when business and labor believe that controls are a temporary phenomenon there is less incentive to incur the moral indignation of friends and neighbors by evasion.

Unfortunately, we cannot provide a happy ending to our story on inflation. The current state of the art does not have the solution to the inflation-unemployment confrontation. Money is at the root of inflation in the long run but not the short run. The Phillips Curve is alive and well in the short run but not the long run. Wage-price controls work in the short run but not the long run. Living with inflation, as suggested by Tobin and Ross, may be a good idea—but for how long?

7

ARE HIGH INTEREST RATES

ALWAYS BAD?

It is time for a pop quiz. Compare yourself with the experts. Check all those you know, way down deep, are more true than false:

High interest rates
( ) result from collusion between Wall Street and Big Business.
( ) make the rich richer and the poor poorer.
( ) create unemployment and cause depression.
( ) raise prices and cause inflation.

We all think we know the answers. But do we? Have we ever really thought them through?

The Conspiratorial Interpretation
of Interest Rates

There is a deep-seated suspicion in American society that conspiracy is everywhere afoot. Television programs are awful because "they" want them that way. Stocks go up or down because "insiders" are rigging the market. Rents are high because the landlords are ganging up on the rest of us. The Yankees always won because that's how "they" wanted it; now "they" don't want it that way any more, so the Yankees lose. The Establishment thinks the New Left is manipulated by a few hard-core conspirators (two SDS members, a Black Panther, a Soviet attaché, and a professor); and the militants think the military-industrial complex (in the person of a general, two corporation presidents, a United States senator, and a professor) is plotting behind closed doors to manipulate everybody else. We've all seen too many Westerns. So why should interest rates be any different?

Insofar as interest rates are concerned, and regardless of the merits of these other matters (although the only one that sounds plausible to us is the one concerning the Yankees), it is in fact extremely doubtful that any one person or group in the United States, aside from perhaps the Federal Reserve and the United States Treasury, has anywhere near enough power even to influence interest rates, much less set them.

That statement may be a slight exaggeration. But even if it is, it is still much closer to reality than the more popular conspiratoral theory of interest rate determination. For the simple reason that in this country there are too many lenders engaged in the business of lending, and therefore too many alternatives open to most would-be borrowers, to make it possible for any tightly knit clique of lenders (or borrowers, for that matter) to control the price of credit. They would love to. Who doubts that? But they are not *able* to. The wish, as 93-year-old George Bernard Shaw commented when he considered marrying Brigitte Bardot, is not always father to the deed.

Suppose that the three largest banks in the United States —the Bank of America, the First National City Bank of

New York, and Chase Manhattan, with aggregate assets amounting to almost $90 billion at the end of 1971 (of total commercial bank assets of $640 billion)—were to decide, in concert, to raise interest rates above prevailing levels during a time when there was *no overall upward pressure on rates.* Could they pull it off?

Not very likely. Quite aside from the antitrust laws, their business customers would simply shift to other banks, or decide to raise their funds in the commercial paper market, or float bonds in the nationwide corporate bond market, or utilize any one of a wide variety of other potential alternatives. Consumers could also shift to another bank, or to a savings and loan association, or to their local credit union. If the three would-be monopolists wanted to continue doing very much business, they would have little choice but to bring their rates back into line.

Even the Federal Reserve does not have enough power to set interest rates at whatever level it pleases, whenever it wishes. The central bank may control the supply of credit, but it does not control the demand, and both are involved in the determination of its price.

The facts of life, in this case at least, are rather prosaic. There is considerable competition in the market for loanable funds: competition among lenders for potential creditworthy borrowers and competition among borrowers for the available supply of funds. Lenders charging more than prevailing rates will price themselves out of the market and lose business to their competitors. Borrowers trying to borrow at cheaper rates will find themselves outbid for funds by others.

The Rich Get Richer and the Poor Get Poorer

Inequality in the distribution of income may possibly be getting worse. However, there is some hopeful evidence to the contrary in a few countries, including the United States, Great Britain, Scandinavia, and Castro's Cuba. But whatever the facts, the fault hardly lies with the interest rate, high or low.

The blame for continued bedrock poverty in the United States might conceivably be attributed to capitalism, but if so—and the evidence is less than convincing—it has little to do with the interest rate. Socialist and communist economies have interest rates just as capitalist ones. Indeed, regardless of the type of economic system, wherever funds are scarce and have alternative immediate as well as future uses there will be interest rates, whatever they are called.

It deserves mention, by the way, that financial institutions *pay out* interest as well as take it in. Currently the largest category of bank costs is interest paid out to depositors, a larger cost item than even wages and salaries. Assuming that all bankers are rich and all depositors poor, an unlikely assumption if there ever was one, the flow of interest on savings deposits—which increases when interest rates rise—redistributes income from the rich to the poor. The financial position of small depositors and bondholders is often ignored when the income-redistribution effects of high interest rates are discussed.

The fact of the matter is that the causes of poverty in this country have little to do with interest rates. The primary reasons for most of our poverty are much less complicated than the intricacies of money, financial markets, or fluctuations in interest rates. The poor get poorer because to a large extent they are elderly or unskilled or black or Puerto

Rican or Mexican-American or Indian. They get poorer because they are elderly and inflation erodes their savings, or because they are unskilled and unable to compete in the job market, or because the skills they do possess have been made obsolete by the onrush of technology.

For many, poverty is quite simply the bitter legacy of several centuries of sharp-edged bigotry; the fruit of persistent, widespread, and systematic prejudice against racial, religious, and nationality minorities in education, housing, and employment. They get poorer not because interest rates are high but because they get third-rate educations in inferior schools, because they are denied access to clean and decent housing, because they encounter a mountainous avalanche of employer discrimination in job advancement and union discrimination in admission and apprentice requirements, because they are tangled up in a topsy-turvy welfare system that penalizes initiative, discourages family ties, and fosters dependency and cynicism.

For the most part, high interest rates are a contrived scapegoat. The elimination of hard-core poverty does not lie in perpetually low interest rates. It lies in an overhaul of our educational system, in adequate job-training programs, in more sensible welfare and social security arrangements, and in the maintenance of a high-employment economy without inflation within which there is full and complete equality of opportunity for everyone. (Will everyone please rise for a singing of our national anthem!)

Do High Interest Rates Create Unemployment?

Tight money and the high interest rates it typically induces are not designed to create unemployment. Tight money is intended to prevent inflation or at least slow it down. How-ever, some object strenuously to its use as an anti-infla-tionary weapon on the grounds that it is a very dangerous instrument that cannot be used in moderation—that if effective at all, it is likely to be *too effective*, setting off a financial crisis and an ensuing recession.

Thus, Alvin Hansen, for years the foremost American Keynesian, wrote in 1949:

> The monetary weapon has the peculiar characteristic that it is scarcely at all effective unless the brakes are applied so vigorously as to precipitate a collapse. Those who glibly talk about controlling inflation by monetary policy have failed to consider that moderate monetary measures by themselves alone are relatively ineffective, while drastic measures may easily turn the economy into a tailspin.

A decade later, in 1959, in a report for the Joint Eco-nomic Committee of the Congress, practically the same thesis was reasserted by Warren Smith, who several years later was to become a member of President Johnson's Council of Economic Advisers: "It is perhaps just as well that monetary controls have not been very effective; if they had been, they might have been disastrous."

And right on schedule, ten years after *that*, in 1969, the same views were put forth by others, particularly the labor unions, as soon as monetary policy began to tighten.

Assessments of monetary policy along these lines are paralyzing. If taken seriously, monetary policy would be employed so gingerly in fighting inflation that it could hardly be anything but useless. We have now had, in the postwar period, more than two decades of more-or-less active countercyclical monetary policy, sometimes devoted to offsetting recession and sometimes to counteracting in-flation. And thus far, tight money, periodically imposed, has not precipitated either Hansen's tailspin or Smith's disaster.

Every economic policy involves some degree of risk. The Federal Reserve might indeed go too far. But on the basis of the record up to now, the potential depression risk involved in actively employing tight money to check inflation appears to be far less than the potential inflation risk of being afraid to ever use monetary policy at all.

In the years before World War II, mass unemployment was the dominant economic problem in this country. In the broad sweep of the postwar period, the major concern has not been depression, but inflation. We can't effectively fight the economic problems of the 1970s, whatever they may be, if we continue to be hypnotized by the problems of the 1930s.

Do High Interest Rates Make Inflation Worse?

Although the announced purpose of tight money is to restrain inflation, complaints against its use have consistently come from critics who believe that high interest rates make inflation *worse* rather than better. Since interest is one of the costs of doing business, it is argued, higher interest rates, like higher wages, tend to *raise* rather than lower prices.

Congressman Wright Patman of Texas is a leading proponent of this point of view, as are spokesmen for organized labor. Surprisingly, there is possibly more truth in this position than in any of the others discussed in this chapter, and it may contain more validity than most professional economists—who refuse to take it seriously and typically dismiss it out of hand—are willing to admit.

Higher interest rates *do* increase costs, and thereby push prices up from the supply side. They also *do* result in larger incomes for lenders, owners of savings deposits, and bond-holders, enabling them to increase their spending, thereby pulling prices up from the demand side. Cost push and demand pull. On the surface, at least, higher interest rates are not so different from higher wage rates. If the latter are inflationary, why not the former?

The standard response to these arguments is that interest is so small an element of business costs, and of income, that higher rates don't matter that much. But such a response raises more questions than it answers. Indeed, it goes so far that it all but destroys the orthodox case for higher interest rates made by the proponents of monetary policy themselves—which is that higher rates lower investment spending, decrease aggregate demand, and thus reduce inflationary pressures. If interest is so minute an element of business costs, then how can higher rates be expected to significantly affect investment spending, as the proponents of monetary policy claim?

The fact is that interest is *not* a negligible item in business costs. In expenditures for long-lived plant or equipment, particularly, it may be a crucial component of costs. For example, if you buy a $20,000 home and get a mortgage for the full amount at 7 percent interest for thirty years, before all is over and done with, you will be paying $28,000 in interest and the $20,000 house will wind up costing you $48,000. If the interest rate increases to 8 percent, your total interest payments will add up to $33,000 and the house will cost you $53,000, almost triple its list price.

Furthermore, interest is no trivial component of national income. In recent years it has been running at about 10 percent of personal after-tax income.

The orthodox response, then, to the "higher interest rates raise prices" argument is wrong. If that were the only answer, the heretics would be far more correct than the traditionalists, even on the traditionalists' own grounds. The answer, if there is any, will have to be found elsewhere.

The answer to the "high interest rates raise prices" school of thought lies in a closer examination of the assumed similarity between the effects of higher wage rates and the effects of higher interest rates. In the previous chapter we pointed out that higher wage rates are inflationary. Wage increases in excess of productivity gains mean higher costs, thereby putting upward cost pressure on prices from the supply side. Higher wages also mean larger incomes for wage-earners, thereby generating an increase in consumer spending that pulls prices up from the demand side. Congressman Patman and others claim that higher interest rates do exactly the same thing. *And Congressman Patman is right.* Higher interest rates *do* raise costs and incomes, and *do* thereby generate cost-push and demand-pull inflationary pressures.

In the previous chapter we also pointed out, however, that wage increases, *alone*, could not fully explain either cost-push or demand-pull inflation. To maintain inflation for any sustained period of time, wage increases must be accompanied by continued injections of new money: permissive increases in the money supply are a necessary condition for the continuation of inflation. If the central bank does *not* increase the money supply, or actually reduces it, inflation will sooner or later peter out, regardless of the strength of unions or the monopoly power of business.

Similarly, high interest rates accompanied by monetary expansion are also inflationary. But rising interest rates attributable to tight money—monetary restriction—are not. The rising interest rates that result from tight money should be equated *not* with higher wages plus an enlarged money supply, which is typically the equation that is implied, but with higher wage rates accompanied by a constant or lower money supply—as if every time wages increased by so many percent, the central bank automatically cut back the rate of growth in the money supply a similar percent. For this, in general terms, is what happens when interest rates rise during a period of *tight* money.

Such higher interest rates, like higher wages under similar circumstances, may raise the price level briefly, but if the central bank sticks to its guns it will not go up far or for long. With a constant or lower money supply, further increases in the price level would be difficult to finance, the higher interest rates will choke off some spending, and sooner or later total expenditures will stop rising. At that point the inflation process will grind to a halt, regardless of the higher costs, as a result of tight monetary policy.

PART III

*Federal Reserve
Policy-making*

8

WHO'S IN CHARGE HERE?

Monetary policy is the responsibility of the Federal Reserve, but to whom is the Federal Reserve responsible?

The answer to that question is so complex that if we successfully unravel it (which is a not too likely prospect), we possibly will have either unveiled one of the great socioeconomic creations in the annals of civilization, comparable to the invention of inside plumbing, or unmasked one of the most devious schemes ever contrived by the mind of man to camouflage the true locus of clandestine power.

According to some, the Federal Reserve is responsible to the Congress. But it is the president, not Congress, who appoints the members of the Board of Governors of the Federal Reserve System, the seven men (never yet a woman) who occupy the stately building at 20th Street and Constitution Avenue, Washington, D.C. The president also selects from among those seven the chairman of the Board of Governors, the principal spokesman for the central bank.

On that basis, one might surmise that the Federal Reserve is responsible to the executive branch of government, in the person of the president and his administration. However, since each member serves a fourteen-year term, the current president can appoint only two of the seven-man Board of Governors, unless there are deaths or resignations. Even the chairman may be the appointee of the previous administration. Furthermore, it is Congress that created the Federal Reserve (not in its own image) in 1913, and it is Congress, not the president, that has the authority to alter its working mandate at any time. In 1935, for example, Congress chose to throw two administration representatives off the Board of Governors—namely, the secretary of the Treasury and the comptroller of the currency, both of whom had been ex officio members—simply because they were representatives of the executive branch.

Others, more cynical, have suggested that the Federal Reserve is mostly responsible to the private banking community, primarily the 6,000 commercial banks that are member banks of the Federal Reserve System. The member banks do in fact choose the presidents of each of the twelve regional Federal Reserve banks, including the president of the most aristocratic one of all, the Federal Reserve Bank of New York. It may or may not be significant that the annual salary of the president of the Federal Reserve Bank of New York is $90,000, while that of the chairman of the Board of Governors in Washington is $42,500.

Who's in charge here? Who, indeed?

Formal Structure

The statutory organization of the Federal Reserve System is a case study in those currently popular concepts, decentralization and the blending of public and private authority. A deliberate attempt was made in the enabling congressional legislation to diffuse power over a broad base —geographically, between the private and public sectors, and even within the government—so that no one man, group, or sector, either inside or outside the government, could exert enough leverage to dominate the thrust of monetary policy.

The Formal Structure and Policy Organization of the Federal Reserve System

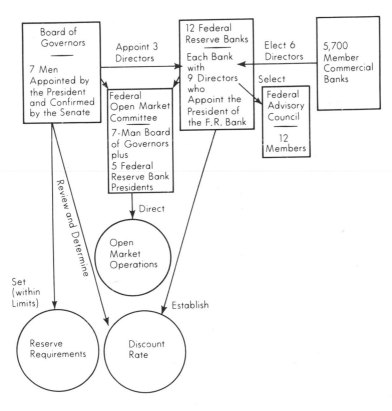

As noted in the formal organizational diagram, above, the Board of Governors of the Federal Reserve System consists of seven members, appointed by the president with the advice and consent of the Senate. In order to prevent presidential board-packing, each member is appointed for a term of fourteen years, with one term expiring at the end of January in each even-numbered year. Furthermore, no two board members may come from the same Federal Reserve District. The chairman of the Board of Governors, chosen from among the seven by the president, serves a four-year term. However, his term is not concurrent with the presidential term, so that an incoming president could find himself saddled with an already appointed chairman for most of his first term in office. The board is independent of the congressional appropriations process and of audit by the government's watchdog, the General Accounting Office, since its operating funds come from the earnings of the twelve regional Federal Reserve banks.

The regional Federal Reserve banks, one in each Federal Reserve District, are geographically dispersed throughout the nation—the Federal Reserve Bank of New York, the Federal Reserve Bank of Kansas City, the Federal Reserve Bank of San Francisco, and so on. Each Federal Reserve Bank is privately owned by the member banks in its district, the very commercial banks it is charged with supervising and regulating. However, the profits accruing to ownership are limited by law to a 6 percent annual dividend on paid-in capital stock. The member bank stockholders elect six of the nine directors of their district Federal Reserve Bank, and the remaining three are appointed from Washington by the Board of Governors. These nine directors, in turn, choose the president of their Federal Reserve Bank, subject to the approval of the Board of Governors.

The directors of each Federal Reserve Bank also select one person, always a commercial banker, to serve on the Federal Advisory Council, a statutory body consisting of one member from each of the twelve Federal Reserve districts. The Federal Advisory Council consults quarterly with the Board of Governors in Washington and makes recommendations regarding the conduct of monetary policy.

Legal authority is similarly diffused with respect to the *execution* of monetary policy, as the diagram indicates. The Board of Governors has the power to set reserve requirements on commercial bank time and demand deposits, for example, but it cannot set them outside the bounds of the specific and rather narrow limits imposed by the Congress (between 3 and 10 percent for time deposits, between 7 and 14 percent for demand deposits at smaller "country" banks, between 10 and 22 percent for demand deposits at larger "city" banks).

Open market operations are directed by a body known as the Federal Open Market Committee (FOMC), composed of the seven-man Board of Governors plus five of the Reserve Bank presidents. Since the members of the Board of Governors are appointed by the White House, and the Reserve Bank presidents are appointed by the directors of each Federal Reserve Bank, who are (six of nine) elected by the member commercial banks, the diffusion of authority over open market operations spans the distance from the White House to the member bank on Main Street. In addition, although the FOMC directs open market operations, they are executed at the trading desk of the Federal Reserve Bank of New York by a gentleman who appears to be simultaneously an employee of the FOMC and the Federal Reserve Bank of New York.

Legal authority over discount rates is even more confusing. Discount rates are "established" every two weeks by the directors of each regional Federal Reserve Bank, but they are subject to "review and determination" by the Board of Governors. The distinction between "establishing" discount rates and "determining" them is a fine line indeed, and it would not be surprising if occasionally confusion arose as to precisely where the final authority and responsibility lie.

The Realities of Power

So much for the Land of Oz. Actually, the facts of life are rather different, as a more realistic diagram, below, illustrates.

By all odds, the dominant figure in the formation and execution of monetary policy is the chairman of the Board of Governors of the Federal Reserve System. He is the most prominent member of the board itself, the most influential member of the FOMC, and generally recognized, by both Congress and the public at large, as *the* spokesman for the Federal Reserve System. Although the Federal Reserve Act appears to put all seven members of the Board of Governors on a more or less equal footing, over the past thirty-five years the strong personalities, outstanding abilities, and determined devotion to purpose of the chairmen—first Marriner S. Eccles, then William McChesney Martin, and now Arthur F. Burns—have made them rather more equal than the others. As adviser to the president, negotiator with Congress, and final authority on appointments throughout the system, with influence over all aspects of monetary policy in his capacity as chairman of both the Board of Governors and the FOMC, the chairman of the Board of Governors for all practical purposes is the embodiment of the central bank in this country.

The other six members of the Board of Governors also exercise a substantial amount of authority, more so than is indicated in the formal paper structure of the system, because with the passage of time primary responsibility for monetary policy has become more centralized and concentrated in Washington. When the Federal Reserve Act was first enacted, in 1913, it was thought that the Federal Reserve System would be mainly a passive service agency, supplying currency when needed, clearing checks, and providing a discount facility for the convenience of the private commercial member banks. At that time there was no conception of monetary policy as an active countercyclical force. Open market operations were unknown and reserve

The Realities of Power within the Federal Reserve System

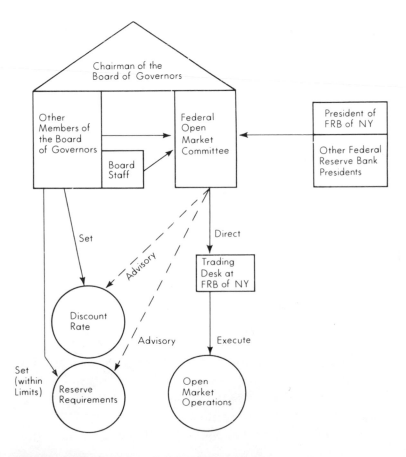

requirements were fixed by law, with no flexibility permitted. Since then, of course, the central bank has shifted from passive accommodation to active regulation, from the performance of regional service functions to the implementation of national economic policy. This shift has been accompanied, naturally enough, by a rise in the power of the centralized Board of Governors and a corresponding decline in the role of the regional Federal Reserve Banks and their "owners," the commercial banks.

It would not be unrealistic to describe the central bank today as being headquartered in Washington, with twelve field offices located throughout the nation. These field offices may be known by the rather imposing name Federal Reserve Bank, but they essentially amount to little more than branches of the Washington headquarters, nevertheless.

Closely related to the Board of Governors in the informal power structure, and deriving influence through that association, is the board's professional staff of economic experts and advisers. The long tenure in the Federal Reserve System of many senior staff economists, their familiarity with Federal Reserve history, and their expertise in monetary analysis give them a power base that is to a large extent founded on the respect with which they, as individuals, are held throughout the system. Through daily consultation with the individual governors and written and oral presentations before each meeting of the FOMC, staff personnel exert an indefinable but significant influence on the ultimate decision-making process.

Aside from the Board of Governors, its chairman and its staff, the only other body playing a major role in Federal Reserve policy-making is the Federal Open Market Committee, which meets every three or four weeks in Washington. Of the twelve members on the FOMC, a majority

of seven are the Board of Governors themselves. The other
five, on a rotating basis, are Reserve Bank presidents. The
president of the Federal Reserve Bank of New York is a
permanent member of the FOMC, and the other eleven
Federal Reserve Bank presidents alternate the remaining
four seats among themselves.   */ 57410*

The statutory authority of the FOMC is confined to the
direction of open market operations, but in recent years it
has become the practice to bring all policy matters under
review at the FOMC meetings. Although only five of the
Reserve Bank presidents are entitled to vote at any one
time, typically all twelve attend every meeting and partici-
pate in the discussion. Thus, potential reserve-requirement
and discount-rate changes are, in effect, decided upon
within the FOMC, with the twelve Reserve Bank presidents participating in an advisory capacity. The Board of
Governors, however, always has the final say on reserve
requirements and discount rates if matters should come to
a showdown, particularly since legal opinion appears to be
that in case of disagreement the board's power to "determine" discount rates overrides the authority of the individual Reserve Banks to "establish" them.

Once the Federal Open Market Committee decides on
the appropriate open market policy, the actual execution
of the policy directive until the next meeting is the responsibility of the account manager at the Federal Reserve
Bank of New York's trading desk. Since the FOMC's instructions are generally couched in rather broad language
—to conduct open market operations so as to attain
"somewhat easier conditions" in the money market, or so
as to "move toward firmer conditions"—the account
manager has to translate these vague instructions into
actual daily purchases and sales of Treasury securities. In
the process, at least a modest amount of leeway and per-

sonal interpretation is inevitable, as we discuss further in Chapter 10.

Like the account manager, the unique position of the president of the Federal Reserve Bank of New York in the hierarchy also stems from his role and status in the nation's financial center. If he is inclined to use this leverage, as Allan Sproul did a decade or two ago and Benjamin Strong before him, the president of the New York Reserve Bank can mount a substantial challenge even to the chairman of the Board of Governors. Since such a challenge would have little legal foundation, it would have to be based on the prestige of the presidency of the Federal Reserve Bank of New York and the forcefulness of the man who holds the position. Both Sproul and Strong were men of exceptional ability and personality.

But where, in the corridors of power, does this leave the member banks, the directors of each Federal Reserve Bank, and the Federal Advisory Council? Pretty much shut out, if the truth be known.

The member banks do indeed "own" their district Federal Reserve Bank, but such stockholding is mostly symbolic and carries with it none of the usual attributes of ownership. The member banks also have a major voice in electing the directors of their Reserve Bank, but the directors in turn have responsibilities that are largely ceremonial. True, they appoint the members of the Federal Advisory Council, but the Federal Advisory Council serves mostly a public relations purpose and has little to do with policy-making. The directors of each Federal Reserve Bank also choose the president of their Reserve Bank, subject to the approval of the Board of Governors. But the "subject to approval" clause has meant, in practice, that the most the directors can really do is submit a list of nominees for the position. On more than one occasion, the choice of the directors of a Federal Reserve Bank has not met with approval from Washington; in such cases, it has become very clear exactly where ultimate authority is lodged.

How Independent the Central Bank?

The fact that ultimate authority over monetary policy resides in Washington brings to the fore the relationship between the central bank and the other branches of government also responsible for overall national economic policy —the Congress and the administration, the latter personified by the president.

The Federal Reserve is a creature of the Congress. The Constitution gives Congress the power "to coin money and regulate the value thereof." On this basis, Congress created the Federal Reserve System as the institution delegated to administer that responsibility on its behalf. Congress requires periodic accountability by the Federal Reserve and has the power to alter or amend the enabling legislation, the Federal Reserve Act, any time it sees fit.

Essentially, Congress has given the Federal Reserve a broad mandate to regulate the monetary system in the public interest and then has stood aside, more or less, and let the monetary authorities pursue this objective on their own and to the best of their abilities. Congress has also attempted to minimize interference on the part of the administration by giving each member of the Board of Governors a fourteen-year term, thereby sharply limiting any one president's influence over the board.

This semiindependent status of the central bank is a source of continuous friction. A small minority of Congress appears to believe that the Federal Reserve has carried its "independence" much too far. There has been some concern over its freedom from congressional appropriations and from standard government audit. Also, the Federal Reserve's responsibility on occasion for tight money and high interest rates has, from time to time, stimulated intensive questioning at congressional hearings, including frequent scoldings of Federal Reserve officials by populist-minded congressmen who get uptight about tight money.

Others, in Congress and out, have complained that the Federal Reserve simply has not done a very good job, that we would all be better off if Congress laid down some guidelines or rules to limit the discretion available to the monetary authorities in conducting their business. We shall discuss such proposals further in Chapter 11.

The relationship between the central bank and the president has also aroused considerable controversy. Many feel that the Federal Reserve should be a part of the administration, responsible to the president, on the grounds that monetary policy is an integral part of national economic policy. Monetary policy should therefore be coordinated at the highest level (that is, by the president), along with fiscal policy, as a component part of the administration's total program for economic growth and stability.

To do otherwise, it is charged, is both undemocratic and divisive. Undemocratic, because monetary policy is too important to be run by an elite group of experts insulated from the political process. Divisive, because monetary and fiscal policy should not work at cross-purposes. Since fiscal policy proposals are clearly within the president's domain, monetary policy should be as well. A Federal Reserve independent of presidential authority conflicts with the administration's responsibility to promulgate and co-ordinate an overall economic program.

On the other hand, the case for central bank independence from the executive branch of government rests on the pragmatic basis that subordination of the central bank to the executive invites excessive money creation and consequent inflation. The charge that an independent Federal Reserve is undemocratic is countered by the reminder that the central bank is still very much responsible to Congress. In addition, the chairman of the Board of Governors confers regularly with the president, the secretary of the Treasury, and the chairman of the president's Council of Economic Advisers.

It is feared by many, and not without historical justification, that if the monetary authority is made the junior partner to the president or the Treasury (the fiscal authority), monetary stability will be sacrificed to the government's revenue needs—that the government will be tempted to seek the easy way out in raising funds, by printing money or borrowing excessively at artificially low interest rates, in preference to the politically more difficult route of raising taxes or cutting back on government spending. The sole purpose of an independent monetary authority, in brief, is to forestall the asserted natural propensity of governments to resort to inflation.

9

INDICATORS AND INSTRUMENTS

The telephone number of Radio City Music Hall at Rocke-feller Center is (212) 757–3100. If you call them, they will be happy to tell you what is going on this week: what picture is playing, at what times, when the stage show begins, just about everything except the personal habits of the Rockettes. The telephone number of the Board of Governors of the Federal Reserve System in Washington is (202) 737–1100. However, if you call *them* to find out what is going on, you will not learn much more than if you dialed the Central Intelligence Agency—(703) 351–1100.

There is nothing cloak-and-dagger about the Federal Reserve. It spews forth an alarming volume of reports, pamphlets, magazines, monographs, and books that explain what central banking is all about. Guided tours and speakers are provided free of charge. Federal Reserve personnel are delighted to discuss in detail why and how they did what they did one, two, or ten years ago. But the one thing they are reluctant to talk about, like central bankers throughout the world, is what they are doing today and what they are going to do tomorrow.

How, then, can we find out what "our central bank," as some affectionately refer to it, is up to? What kind of monetary policy is being featured this week—easy or tight, pinch or squeeze? Will it be held over next week by popular demand or replaced by a coming attraction?

To judge by the press, many financial observers rely on movements in the discount rate to indicate the current stance and future course of monetary policy. A change in the discount rate is heralded on the front page of the *New York Times* and solemnly announced in respectful tones by Walter Cronkite on the evening news. It is implied that when the Federal Reserve raises the discount rate, tight money is being ushered in, and when the discount rate is lowered, easy money is entering from the wings.

On the other hand, most Federal Reserve officials and academic economists agree that the discount rate is the *least* powerful of all the monetary instruments, a follower rather than a leader of monetary policy. So what indicators should we study? In order to assess the importance or unimportance of the discount rate and other indicators of central bank actions and intentions, let us first examine discount policy in some detail and then compare it with the other major tools of monetary policy—open market operations and reserve requirements.

How Important Is the Discount Rate?

One of the primary functions of a central bank, perhaps *the* primary function, has always been to stand ready at all times to provide liquidity to the economy in case of financial stress or crisis. As the ultimate source of liquidity, the central bank is responsible for promptly supplying money on those rare but crucial occasions when the economy threatens to break down for lack of funds. For this reason, the central bank has traditionally been called the "lender of last resort" in emergency situations. In more ordinary circumstances, it also lends funds to banks that are temporarily short of reserves. When the central bank lends, for whatever purpose, the rate of interest it charges is called the discount rate.

The discount rate was considered the main instrument of central banking throughout the nineteenth century and for the first three decades of the twentieth. It reached its apogee in prestige in 1931, when England's Macmillan Committee, somewhat carried away by the splendor of it all, reported that the discount rate "is an absolute necessity for the sound management of a monetary system, and is a most delicate and beautiful instrument for the purpose."

The long tradition behind discounting and the corollary importance of the discount rate stem from the fact that until the mid-1920s it was virtually the only means available to the central bank to accomplish its purposes. Now, of course, with other instruments also at the Federal Reserve's disposal, the relative role of discounting has declined noticeably.

It should be mentioned at the outset that discount policy has two dimensions: one is *price*, the discount rate, the rate of interest the Federal Reserve charges commercial banks when they borrow from the Fed; the other is Federal Reserve surveillance over the *amount* that each bank is borrowing. Thus, one obvious flaw in using the discount rate alone as an indicator of monetary policy is that the rate might remain unchanged while the Federal Reserve employs more stringent (or more lenient) surveillance procedures. Monetary policy could thereby become tighter or easier, even through discount policy, but without any change in the discount rate.

The objective of raising the discount rate is just what the Federal Reserve says it is: to discourage commercial banks from borrowing at the Federal Reserve. When banks borrow from the Federal Reserve, their reserves increase and on that base they can expand their loans and investments and thereby the money supply. Less borrowing at the Federal Reserve because of a higher discount rate thus means less bank lending to business, a smaller growth in the money supply, and higher interest rates generally.

This process, it should be noted, provides no *direct* connection between changes in the discount rate and changes in market interest rates. The effects of a change in the discount rate are seen as operating through the mechanism of changes in bank reserves and the money supply, just as is the case with open market operations and changes in reserve requirements. (However, as we point out in the next section, the magnitude of the effect on reserves of a change in the discount rate is minute, compared with the reserve effects of the two other tools available to the Federal Reserve.)

And yet, there does appear to be a connection between the discount rate and market interest rates. As can be seen in the following diagram, a close relationship exists between the discount rate and interest rates on short-term money-market instruments, such as Treasury bills, and also between the discount rate and the prime bank lending rate, the interest rate that banks charge their best business customers.

Careful examination, however, reveals that changes in Treasury-bill yields typically *precede* changes in the discount rate. Treasury-bill yields rise, probably because of Federal Reserve open market operations, and then—after they have risen quite a while and often quite a bit—the discount rate moves up. Or bill rates fall and then the discount rate is lowered. In other words, a change in the discount rate is likely to come *after* a basic switch in monetary

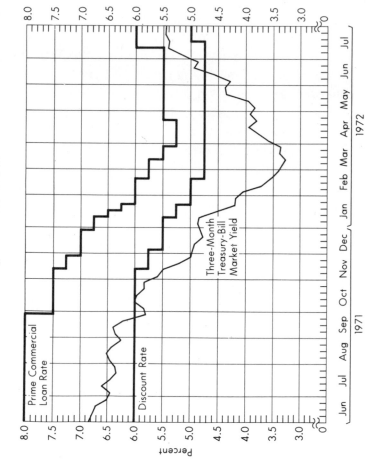

Togetherness, 1970-71

policy has already occurred; it verifies the switch and reinforces it, but does not signal it.

One possible way that changes in the discount rate might directly affect market interest rates is through the "announcement effect" produced when a discount-rate change comes unexpectedly. An unanticipated rise in the discount rate is likely to lead bondholders to expect tight money and higher interest rates (lower bond prices). They sell bonds to avoid capital losses, thus hastening the drop in bond prices and the rise in interest rates.

The key, of course, is that the rise in the discount rate under such circumstances generates expectations regarding future interest rates. But if the public had already observed tightening in the credit markets prior to the change in the discount rate, the actual announcement itself would produce very little reaction. In fact, the bond markets might be relieved of uncertainty, and interest rates might fall.

In any event, the bulk of the evidence suggests that while there may be some cause-and-effect connection between changes in the discount rate and changes in market interest rates, through expectations, for the most part the relationship is indirect—through changes in bank reserves and the money supply. It also bears repeating that typically a change in the discount rate comes after, not before, a basic shift in monetary policy. It confirms what is going on but does not anticipate it. As an indicator, therefore, it is comparable to a fighter who learns his opponent's right cross is on the way when it crashes into his nose.

In an effort to keep the discount rate in closer touch with other short-term rates, there was a change in the administration of the discount rate late in 1970. During the 1960s, changes in the discount rate were made rather infrequently, a pattern that was mirrored by the prime rate charged by commercial banks to their best customers. During the ten years from 1960 until 1970 the discount rate was changed a total of twelve times and the prime rate was changed a total of sixteen times. (In fact, much of the impact of tight money during that period was transmitted to the prime customers of banks by changes in compensating balances —the portion of a loan that must be held on deposit at the bank—that were required of business firms, and by changes in the standards as to who qualified for the prime rate. Thus, even the comovement in the discount rate and the prime rate was somewhat illusory, since the effective prime rate changed even though the posted rate remained fixed.)

To avoid the uncertain announcement effects associated with large and infrequent changes, the Federal Reserve embarked on a course of altering the discount rate more frequently and in smaller steps. During the fourteen months from November 1970 through December 1971 the discount rate was changed eight times, only four less than during the entire 1960–70 period. Similarly, the prime rate was changed a total of twenty-three times during that period, seven more times than during the entire decade of the 1960s.

The discount rate now follows the movements in short-term rates, especially the Treasury bill rate, even more closely than before. It is clear that the Federal Reserve prefers to get changes in the discount rate off the front pages of the *New York Times* and into the anonymity of the interest rate quotations in the financial section (which happens to be close to the sports section anyway, allowing you to throw away the first section of the paper). Some commercial banks have tied the prime rate to other short-term rates for similar reasons—so that the prime rate no longer has the appearance of an administered rate but rather moves up and down with impersonal market forces.

Discount Rate versus Reserve Requirements versus Open Market Operations

If changes in the discount rate exert their main effects via bank reserves and the money supply, it is relevant to compare them in this respect with the other tools of monetary policy—changes in reserve requirements and open market operations.

What proportion of member-bank reserves is attributable to the discounting process, to member banks' borrowing the reserves from the Federal Reserve? In 1950, total member-bank reserves were about $17 billion; less than half a billion of these reserves were acquired through the discount process. In 1972, member-bank reserves totaled about $33 billion; about $200 million were due to borrowing from the Federal Reserve.

Over the entire twenty-year period of the 1950s and 1960s, borrowings from the Federal Reserve averaged about half a billion dollars annually. Even at its occasional peak levels of around $1.5 billion, discounting never provided as much as 10 percent of total bank reserves and usually the percentage was much less—on average about 2 or 3 percent.

The Federal Reserve does *not* use discount policy as a primary tool for changing bank reserves. For one thing, the initiative for discounting lies with the banks, not with the Federal Reserve. The Federal Reserve can lower the discount rate, but this does not force the banks to increase their borrowings. A change in the discount rate affects only those banks that are in debt to the Federal Reserve, or that consider such borrowing to be a likely source of funds. Many banks never borrow from the Federal Reserve except in dire emergency.

Reserve-requirement changes, on the other hand, have an extremely powerful impact on bank-reserve positions and the money supply. A small change in the required reserve ratio instantly produces a rather large change in bank excess reserves. The April 1969 increase of one-half of one percentage point in required reserves against demand deposits, for example, immediately shifted $650 million of reserves from the excess category, where they could have been used as a basis for loan and deposit expansion, to the required category, where for all practical purposes they were immobilized.

Because the impact is so powerful, so blunt, so immediate, and so widespread, the Federal Reserve uses its authority to change reserve requirements only sparingly, particularly during tight money periods when increases in reserve requirements would be appropriate. An increase in reserve requirements reduces commercial bank profitability, since banks then must hold a larger percentage of their assets in reserve balances that earn no interest. As membership in the Federal Reserve System is voluntary (except for banks with national charters), the Federal Reserve is not eager to discourage membership by raising reserve requirements too frequently. The "harsh hand of the Fed" is most evident when tight money is executed through higher reserve requirements. Since 1951, reserve requirements against demand deposits have been increased only five times, whereas they have been lowered on nine occasions.

After all is said and done, the day-by-day standby of

monetary policy, in good times and bad, is open market operations. The purchase or sale of government securities can be undertaken in large or small amounts, as the Federal Reserve chooses. The impact is fairly prompt; it is possible to proceed gradually and to reverse field rapidly.

One reason market interest rates change before the discount rate changes is because the Federal Reserve has already been active with open market operations. When the Federal Reserve alters the direction of monetary policy, it is open market operations that typically lead the way. It is also open market operations that do the brunt of the work as the new policy gathers momentum, with back-up support where necessary and appropriate from the discount rate and reserve requirements.

A Pride of Lions, a Gaggle of Geese, and a Plethora of Indicators

Unfortunately, since open market operations are so unobtrusive, the search for reliable indicators of what the central bank is up to becomes more difficult than ever. The discount rate is generally not too helpful a guide to what the Federal Reserve is doing, except as confirmation of a change in monetary policy that has already occurred. A change in the direction of monetary policy can occur without any change in the discount rate, and conversely a change in the discount rate does not normally initiate a change in Federal Reserve policy.

Reserve requirement changes are not of much assistance because they are used so seldom. Paradoxically, open market operations are not very helpful for the opposite reason—they are used too frequently.

Weekly data on Federal Reserve open market operations are released every Thursday afternoon and published in Friday's papers. But the knowledge that the Federal Reserve bought or sold so many government securities during any one week, or even over a succession of weeks, is in itself of limited value; the transactions may have been made simply to offset some "outside" factors that were affecting bank reserves, such as a seasonal inflow of currency, changes in the Treasury's cash balances, or any of a multitude of other possibilities. (You can get more details on some of the mechanics of open market operations—if such things turn you on—in the next chapter.)

Since it is widely understood that weekly data on open market operations alone give an inadequate picture of what is going on, many financial observers rely more on movements in interest rates for clues to the current stance of monetary policy. Of all yields, the one most quickly responsive to monetary policy is probably the rate on short-term Treasury bills.

However, as reliable indicators of what the central bank is doing, interest rates have serious limitations. To Monetarists, of course, as we saw in Chapter 4, they are irrelevant. Aside from that, it should be obvious that they are susceptible to change for reasons other than Federal Reserve policy; this makes it dangerous to read them as though they were determined exclusively by the Federal Reserve. The central bank has a substantial influence over the supply of credit, but only limited influence over the demand for it, so that interest rates may fluctuate for reasons that have nothing to do with the Federal Reserve's actions. Tight money generally means a rise in interest rates, but a rise in interest rates does not necessarily mean tight money. Indeed, as we saw in Chapter 4, excessively *easy* money might also produce a rise in interest rates.

Given the shortcomings of all the "orthodox" indicators —the discount rate, open market transactions, and the behavior of interest rates—the Federal Reserve, always helpful, releases what it calls a Reserve Report each Thursday afternoon along with the data on open market operations. The Reserve Report presents current statistics on a wide variety of alternative indicators. You can take your pick!

It lists weekly figures on all of the following: the monetary base, total member-bank reserves, the volume of member-bank discounting from the Federal Reserve, net free reserves, the money supply, the money supply plus time deposits, business loans at large commercial banks, and the bank credit proxy.

All these are self-explanatory except perhaps the monetary base, net free reserves, and the bank credit proxy. The monetary base is defined as total member-bank reserves plus currency outstanding. Net free reserves equals member-bank excess reserves less their borrowings from the Federal Reserve; when borrowings exceed excess reserves, it is usually called net borrowed reserves. The bank credit proxy is total deposits at member banks. It is employed as an early indicator of developing trends in bank credit, since data on deposits become available earlier than data on bank loans and investments.

With this smorgasbord of indicators, plus the orthodox ones that are on the back burner, you can select those that best suit your individual taste. As is obvious from Chapter 4, a Monetarist will lean toward the money supply in one form or another, a Keynesian toward interest rates, bank credit, and business loans. An eclectic will stuff himself on a little bit of everything, and if life becomes more complicated that way he has only himself to blame.

Free reserves attained some degree of popularity a few years ago but have recently fallen from favor. The main trouble is that a given level of free reserves is compatible with many different levels of the money supply and bank credit. The figure for free reserves has fluctuated within roughly the same limits for the past twenty years, while the money supply and bank credit have grown considerably during that interval.

At the same time as the Monetarists are downgrading interest rates as indicators of Federal Reserve policy, because they are not under the firm control of the central bank, Keynesians are saying the same thing about the money supply—that it is influenced by commercial bank behavior in conjunction with swings in economic activity, and that it can be controlled only imperfectly by the Federal Reserve. For example, as interest rates on bank loans and investments rise (relative to the discount rate) during a business upswing, banks borrow more from the discount window, expand their loans, and increase the money supply. Similarly, as interest rates fall, perhaps because of a slowdown in economic activity, banks repay their borrowings at the Federal Reserve, reduce their loans, and contract the money supply.

If it is the central bank that is solely responsible for changes in the the money supply, then it is a good indicator of Federal Reserve policy. But if the money supply can change regardless of Federal Reserve intentions, then using it as an indicator is likely to throw you off the track. In order to save the money supply as an indicator of monetary policy, Monetarists Karl Brunner and Allan Meltzer have marshaled statistical evidence showing that it is Federal Reserve actions—open market operations and reserve-requirement changes—that are the main cause of movements in the money supply. As a back-up, however, they propose the monetary base as an alternative indicator, a first cousin to the money supply but somewhat more directly under the Federal Reserve's thumb.

For other Federal Reservologists, the monetary base is still influenced too much by non–Federal Reserve factors. The public by and large determines the amount of currency in circulation. Removing it from the monetary base leaves us with total reserves as the indicator. For still others, including the architects of the Federal Reserve–MIT–Penn model, total reserves must be purged of reserves arising from member bank borrowing at the discount window—leaving us with unborrowed reserves to chart the course. Finally, the Federal Reserve itself added to the confusion (purposely?) by announcing early in 1972 that it had begun using reserves available to support private nonbank deposits (RPDs) as an operating target; this measure removes from total reserves those reserves needed for U.S. Government deposits and interbank deposits, neither of which is included as part of the money supply. By this time, things have clearly gotten out of hand as far as the Monetarists are concerned, and they disassociate themselves from anything further removed from the money supply than the monetary base.

Confused? Read on.

Some Helpful Hints

Where does all this leave someone who is trying to make an honest buck deciphering and predicting the posture of monetary policy? Instead of responding with a cliché (as is our custom)—such as "Life is tough for everyone"—we offer a series of helpful hints (HHs) to aid in interpreting Federal Reserve behavior.

(1) Divide the indicators into two groups. One: *monetary aggregates*—including the money supply (M1), money supply plus time deposits (M2), the bank credit proxy, the monetary base, total reserves. Two: *money market conditions*—especially interest rates on Treasury bills and the federal funds rate (the rate quoted on overnight loans of reserves between banks).

(2) Do not conclude that because there has been an increase in the aggregates that monetary policy is embarked on a wild expansion. The money supply, for example, must increase with a growing economy in order to provide funds for the increased transactions associated with a larger GNP. The money supply has, in fact, increased in every year since 1952 save one (1960), although it can and has declined over shorter intervals (say three or six months).

(3) Try to judge whether the aggregates, say the money supply, are growing faster than normal (expansionary policy) or slower than normal (restrictive policy). What is normal? The money supply grew at an annual rate of 3.1 percent during the twenty years from 1952 through 1971. From 1952 through 1965, however, its growth was only 2.3 percent a year, and from 1966 through 1971 it was 5.6 percent. Take your pick.

(4) If interest rates are falling at the same time as the aggregates are increasing at a faster-than-normal rate, it is a good bet that the Federal Reserve has embarked on a course of monetary expansion. And if interest rates are rising at the same time as the aggregates are growing at a slower-than-normal rate, it is an equally good bet that the Federal Reserve has begun to exercise restraint.

(5) The Federal Reserve publishes the minutes of the FOMC meetings with a three-month lag. Read them. If the Federal Reserve decided on increased monetary ease three months ago and your reading of the indicators shows it has

not succeeded, look for signs of further easing. If tighter monetary policy was decided upon three months ago and your reading of the indicators shows that the Federal Reserve hasn't succeeded—call your broker and sell (see Chapter 14 first).

Naturally, we assume no responsibility for the misfortunes brought down upon you when following these HHs. But we insist on 10 percent of the profits. For those of you who prefer to construct your own "super indicator" for monetary policy, you are invited to read the next chapter, which explains how to read the directive issued at the FOMC meetings and also treats you to a detailed look at the mechanics of open market operations.

10

THE NUTS AND BOLTS OF

MONETARY POLICY

At 11:10 in the morning of each business day, a long-distance conference call takes place among three men: Alan Holmes, the manager of the System Open Market Account, who is located in the Federal Reserve Bank of New York; a member of the Board of Governors in Washington, D.C.; and a president of one of the other Federal Reserve banks currently serving on the Federal Open Market Committee. The job of the account manager is to carry out open market operations for the purpose of implementing the monetary policy directive issued at the last meeting of the FOMC. Each morning he reviews the operations planned for the day via the telephone hookup.

Although we have never listened in to what is said during one of these calls, we can make a pretty good guess at the conversation. With a little imagination, we have been able to reconstruct what might be said, much as sports commentators are able to surmise what is said at those all-important conferences between the quarterback and his coach in the closing minutes of a game, or the even more important huddle between a pitcher and catcher with men on second and third and none out. It probably goes something like this:

OPERATOR: San Francisco and Washington are standing by, New York. Will you deposit $3.35, please?

NEW YORK: You mean it's our turn to pay? Hold on a minute, operator, we don't seem to have enough change here.

WASHINGTON: Hello. This is Chairman Burns on the line.

NEW YORK: Could you spell that for me, please?

WASHINGTON: C-H-A-I-R-M-A-N.

NEW YORK: Oh, it's you, Dr. Burns. What's on your mind?

SAN FRANCISCO: Hello? Hello? Have I been cut off?

WASHINGTON: Mr. Account Manager, we are very unhappy with the way you have been carrying out open market operations. You have not been implementing the directive issued by the FOMC. The directive said "*somewhat* more moderate ease in the money market" and not "somewhat more moderate ease in the money market."

NEW YORK: Those sound fairly close to me, sir.

WASHINGTON: This is outrageous. It's the second time that you have failed to take proper account of an italicized *somewhat*. I think you need a vacation.

NEW YORK: Thank you, sir.

SAN FRANCISCO: Hello? Hello? When do we start?

If you think that we have wrongfully portrayed the plight of the account manager—implying that he is expected to be both a financial wizard and a biblical exegete—a reading of some of the FOMC directives would convince you otherwise.

The manager of the System Open Market Account does, of course, have a more precise idea of what the FOMC would like to see in terms of interest rates and monetary aggregates, but such information is, for the most part, presented orally and is not part of the FOMC directive. The primary thrust of monetary policy is summarized in the FOMC directive. Since the directive plays a key role in guiding the execution of monetary policy, let us take a more detailed look at how it is formulated; and since it is published with a three-month delay, let us also see how it should be interpreted. After examining the directive, we can then return to the open market operations used in carrying it out.

The FOMC Directive

The Federal Open Market Committee meets about once every three or four weeks. At the beginning of each meeting, the staff of the FOMC, comprised of economists from the board of governors and the district Federal Reserve banks, presents a review of recent economic and financial developments—what is happening to prices, unemployment, the balance of payments, interest rates, money supply, bank credit, and so on. Projections are also made for the months ahead. The meeting then proceeds to a discussion among the committee members; each expresses his views on the current economic and financial scene and proposes appropriate monetary policies.

The FOMC directive, embodying the committee's decision on the desired posture of monetary policy until the next meeting, is voted on toward the end of each meeting, with dissenting votes recorded for posterity. If economic conditions are proceeding as had been expected and the current stance of monetary policy is still appropriate, the previous directive may remain unaltered. If conditions change, the directive is modified accordingly.

In the past few years the FOMC directive has usually consisted of two paragraphs. More recently it has been expanded to four paragraphs. The first two paragraphs summarize current economic and financial conditions. The third paragraph states the current objectives of the FOMC with respect to economic growth, inflation, employment, and price stability. The last paragraph contains instructions to the account manager for carrying out open market operations until the next FOMC meeting.

The statement of FOMC objectives in the third paragraph usually begins with a reference to the economic and financial developments reviewed at the meeting and summarized in the first two paragraphs. For example, at the meeting held on 18 April 1972 the goals of the FOMC were stated as follows:

In light of the foregoing developments, it is the policy of the Federal Open Market Committee to foster financial conditions conducive to sustainable real economic growth and increased employment, abatement of inflationary pressures, and attainment of reasonable equilibrium in the country's balance of payments.

While the statement of goals does not contain everything—we know, after all, that the FOMC is not trying to eliminate congestion on the country's highways—it does include virtually every objective of stabilization policy. This statement of goals is rarely changed significantly. During the second half of 1969, a period of extremely contractionary monetary policy, the word *abatement* was replaced by *reduction* before *of inflationary pressures*, and the entire phrase appeared as the first goal.

The last paragraph is aimed at instructing the account manager how to conduct open market operations in order to implement the policy specified in the third paragraph. The operating instructions from the meeting on 18 April 1972 were as follows:

To implement this policy, while taking account of capital market developments and the forthcoming Treasury financing, the Committee seeks to achieve bank reserve and money market conditions that will support somewhat more moderate growth in monetary aggregates over the months ahead.

No, we have not left anything out. That's it. In fact, this particular directive is quite explicit. It indicates a change in monetary policy. The FOMC wants to see *somewhat more moderate* [our italics] growth in monetary aggregates."

Changed Emphasis in the Directive

The emphasis in the directive just cited is clearly on monetary aggregates. It wasn't always that way. In fact, until 1966 the directive to the account manager was couched solely in terms of money market conditions—easier or firmer. Free reserves and short-term interest rates ruled the day, especially the Treasury bill rate and the federal funds rate (the rate charged on reserves lent from one bank to another, usually on an overnight basis).

In 1966, however, the directive was altered to include what was called a proviso clause. The account manager was directed, for example, "to conduct open market operations with a view towards somewhat firmer conditions in the money market, *provided* [our italics] that bank credit was not deviating significantly from projections." At the first meeting in 1970, the monetary aggregates in the directive were expanded to include money as well as bank credit in the proviso clause. At the third meeting in 1970, the monetary aggregates finally were put on a par with money market conditions. The committee expressed a desire to seek "moderate growth in money and bank credit over the months ahead" as well as "money market conditions consistent with that objective." Then, early in 1972, the

FOMC added reserves—or, more precisely, reserves available to support private nonbank deposits (RPDs)—as an operating target along with money market conditions, both of which are to be used to achieve a desired pattern of growth in monetary aggregates.

What's happened? Has the Federal Reserve Bank of St. Louis taken over the entire system? Are we all Monetarists now?

Undoubtedly, one of the reasons for the new emphasis on monetary aggregates stems from the increased empirical evidence that the money supply *does* have a significant impact on economic activity. But there is a more fundamental reason for paying more attention to the monetary aggregates. In its usual posture of deep humility, the Federal Reserve has refused to declare either interest rates or the money supply as the supreme channel through which monetary policy influences real economic activity. As the Federal Reserve sees it, concentrating solely on money market conditions and interest rates can lead to uncontrolled and even perverse movements in the monetary aggregates. Similarly, by focusing only on the money supply and related aggregates, interest rates are seen as subject to wider fluctuations than otherwise. Furthermore, in a world of uncertainty, the Federal Reserve can never be perfectly sure of the source of the decline in economic activity that it seeks to prevent, or the cause of the inflationary pressures it seeks to thwart. Under such circumstances, it feels obliged to focus on *both* monetary aggregates *and* interest rates in the formulation and execution of monetary policy.

These points are sufficiently important to warrant further elaboration by way of some examples. Assume that a decline in economic activity is on the horizon, precipitated by a reduction in business investment spending. The correct course to follow would be expansionary monetary policy: lower interest rates, increase the rate of growth in the monetary aggregates to pump liquidity into the economy, and thereby thwart the impending contraction with both barrels. If the manager of the System Open Market Account looked at interest rates as his only guideline in conducting open market operations, he would observe a fall in interest rates simply because business firms have decided to spend less, borrow less, and because there is a diminished need for cash with a decline in economic activity. He may do nothing, since interest rates are already falling, in which case the aggregates do not increase at all.

Or, if the decline in economic activity is sufficiently great and interest rates fall by more than the FOMC had anticipated, he may even engage in some open market *sales*, thereby lessening the decline in rates but *lowering* the monetary aggregates. By requiring, under such circumstances, faster growth in the aggregates as a target of monetary policy, the FOMC guards against such a perverse outcome.

Suppose, on the other hand, that the decline in economic activity is precipitated by an increased demand for liquidity by households—they want to hold a greater percentage of their portfolio in the form of cash. This would lead to less spending by households, less lending by households, hence higher interest rates, and on both counts lower economic activity. The correct course to pursue is, once again, expansionary monetary policy to increase the aggregates at a faster rate in order to provide for the increased demand for liquidity and in order to lower interest rates to encourage spending. If the manager of the Open Market Account has learned his lesson from the previous example and therefore concentrates only on the aggregates, he will engage in open market purchases to expand the money supply. But if households' demand for liquidity is increasing at a faster rate, their spending will still decline, they will lend less, interest rates will continue to rise, and the contraction in economic activity will not be prevented. By requiring, under such circumstances, lower interest rates as a target of monetary policy, the FOMC guards against such errors.

As long as there is uncertainty over the cause of fluctuations in economic activity, *both* interest rates and monetary aggregates must be used as targets of monetary policy. A Monetarist places more emphasis on the aggregates, since as we saw in Chapter 3 he views velocity and the public's demand for liquidity as relatively stable and predictable. Keynesians rely more on interest rate targets because they are less convinced of a stable demand for liquidity and a predictable velocity. The Federal Reserve—also known as the Great Compromiser—uses both. The account manager —if he wants to keep his job—also uses both. It is now time to see how he does it.

The Operating Room

Open market operations are performed in a well-guarded room within a fortress-like building in the heart of the nation's financial center. The Federal Reserve Bank of New York, designated by the FOMC as its operating arm, is located on Liberty Street only three blocks from Wall Street. This location permits Alan Holmes, the manager of the Federal Reserve System Open Market Account, to be in close contact with the government securities dealers with whom the Federal Reserve System engages in purchases and sales of securities. Every morning of the workweek he meets with one or more of the securities dealers and gets the "feel of the market," as the opening handshakes (firm or limp? dry or sweaty palms?) telegraph whether the market is likely to be a tic tighter or easier. On occasion Holmes has been known to shock the market by the judicious use of one of those little hand buzzers (the kind you get in novelty shoppes).

Feedback from the securities dealers is only one component of the vast array of data and information marshaled by the account manager in mapping his plans for open market operations on any given day. The starting point, of course, is the directive issued by the FOMC at its last meeting. This expression of the proposed stance of monetary policy, together with a more precise range of desired movements in money market conditions and the monetary aggregates conveyed orally by the FOMC staff, provide the ultimate target for open market operations. The account manager must still decide, however, how much to sell or buy, to or from whom, and when.

Money market conditions (particularly short-term interest rates) and monetary aggregates are directly affected by the reserves available to the banking system. Each workday morning, a little after 9:30, the account manager receives a report on the reserve position of the banking system as of the night before. A sensitive indicator of pressure in this market is provided by the federal funds rate.

A little later in the morning—but before the 11:10 conference call—the account manager is provided with a detailed projection by the research staff. It covers movements in various items that can affect the reserve position of the banking system—including currency holdings of the public, deposits in foreign accounts at the Federal Reserve Banks, and other technical factors. A change in any of these can cause reserves to go up or down and thereby affect bank lending capabilities, interest rates, and growth in the money supply. For example, as the public cashes checks in order to hold more currency, commercial banks must pay out vault cash and thereby suffer a loss in reserves. As foreign accounts at Federal Reserve banks increase—that is, as they present checks for payment drawn against commercial banks—reserves of commercial banks are transferred to foreign accounts.

A call is also made to the U.S. Treasury to ascertain what is likely to happen to Treasury balances in tax and loan accounts at commercial banks—deposits of the U.S. Government generated by tax payments of the public and receipts from bond sales—and to find out what is likely to happen to Treasury balances at the Federal Reserve banks, from which most Government expenditures are made. As funds are shifted from Treasury tax and loan accounts in commercial banks to Treasury balances at the Federal Reserve, the commercial banking system loses reserves.

By 11:00 A.M. the account manager has a good idea of money market conditions, including what is happening to interest rates, and of anticipated changes in the reserve position of the banking system. He also knows what the FOMC directive calls for. If the FOMC had asked for moderate growth in reserves in order to sustain moderate growth in the aggregates, and all of the other factors just discussed are expected to pour a large volume of reserves into the banking system, the account manager may decide that open market *sales* are necessary in order to prevent an excessive (more than moderate) expansion in reserves. If, on the other hand, he expects to find reserves going up too little or even declining as a result of these other forces, he may engage in significant open market purchases. It is now clear why knowledge that the Federal Reserve bought or sold so much or so little government securities on a given day or during a given week, in itself tells us almost nothing about the overall posture or intent of monetary policy.

At the 11:10 conference call with a member of the Board of Governors in Washington and one of the Federal Reserve Bank presidents, Alan Holmes outlines his plan of action for the day and explains the reasons for his particular strategy. Once his decision is confirmed, the purchase or sale of securities (usually Treasury bills) takes place. The account manager instructs the traders in the trading room of the Federal Reserve Bank of New York to call the twenty or so government securities dealers and ask them for firm bids for stated amounts of specific maturities of government securities (in the case of an open market sale) or for their selling price quotations for stated amounts of specific maturities (in the case of an open market purchase). While the Federal Reserve does not engage in open market operations in order to make a profit, it still insists on getting the most for its money, and it is assured of that by vigorous competition among the various dealers in government securities.

It takes no more than thirty minutes for the trading desk to complete its "go-around" of the market and to execute the open market purchase or sale. By 12:30 the account manager and his staff are back to watching the situation and, if necessary, buying or selling additional amounts of government securities to implement the original objective.

Much is left to the judgment of the account manager, even with all of the double-checking with other parts of the Federal Reserve System. By and large, Alan Holmes receives high marks for his job, despite the errors that inevitably enter any human undertaking. He is also a very pleasant fellow. There are some, however, who would have him, as well as (or especially) the FOMC, replaced by a computer, an automatic telephone, and a disembodied voice that periodically calls out orders to buy or sell $200, $300, or $400 million worth of government securities. The reasons for such an Orwellian prescription for the Federal Reserve are discussed in the next chapter.

11

SHOULD A ROBOT REPLACE

THE FEDERAL RESERVE?

Some Monetarists, most notably Milton Friedman, have abandoned countercyclical stabilization policy altogether. They never had any use for fiscal policy to begin with, and the issue of time lags in the impact of monetary policy has led them to jettison countercyclical monetary policy as well. In Chapter 5, we noted that time lags do indeed make the implementation of monetary policy potentially hazardous.

"Countercyclical" monetary policy means leaning against the prevailing economic winds: easy money in recessions, to get the economy on the move again; tight money when there is a boom, to slow it down. In its most naive form, however, countercyclical monetary policy tends to ignore the complications bred by time lags.

Assume that the Federal Reserve forecasts a recession due six months from now. If the forecast is correct, and if a current expansion in the money supply would have an impact six months hence, well and good. But what if the Federal Reserve's crystal ball is not that clear, and it is more than a year before the main impact of today's monetary policy is reflected in the economy? Then the effects of today's expansionary monetary policy are likely to be felt after the economy has passed the trough and is already on its way up.

As the accompanying diagram illustrates, the impact of today's easy money may exacerbate tomorrow's inflation. This is Milton Friedman's explanation for the rampant inflation of 1969; the rapid rate of growth in the money supply in 1968, intended to forestall recession, lit the fuse of the inflationary time bomb that exploded the following year. Tight money will have similarly delayed effects; it may be imposed with the best of intentions, to curtail a boom, but its real impact, being long delayed, might accentuate a recession. Monetary policy will be a destabilizer rather than a stabilizer.

On these grounds—the precarious nature of economic forecasting and the alleged length, variability, and unpredictability of the time lags involved—Friedman and some other Monetarists have given up on orthodox monetary policy. Friedman argues that the economy has been and is now inherently stable, and that it would automatically tend

Friedman's Alleged Perverse Effects of Countercyclical Monetary Policy

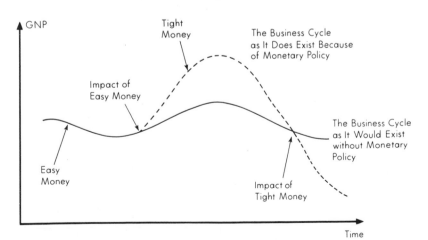

to stay on a fairly straight course if only it were not being almost continuously knocked off the track by erratic or unwise monetary policies. Conclusion: quarantine the central bank. The best stabilization policy is no stabilization policy at all.

Rules versus Discretion

What Professer Friedman proposes instead is that the Federal Reserve be instructed by Congress to follow a fixed long-run rule: Increase the money supply at a steady and inflexible rate, month in and month out, year in and year out, regardless of current economic conditions. Set the money supply on automatic pilot and then leave it alone.

The specific rule would depend on the definition of the money supply adopted; increase the money supply by 3 percent a year if it is defined in the conventional way as demand deposits plus currency, by 4 percent a year if time deposits in commercial banks are added in as well. In either case, the particular number itself is not so important to Friedman as that once it is decided upon it be left alone thereafter. No tinkering!

The 3 (or 4) percent figure is intended to keep prices stable and employment high by allowing aggregate demand to grow secularly at the same rate as the growth in the economy's real productive capacity. It is also supposed to compensate, according to Friedman, for a long-term gradual downtrend in velocity (although, in fact, velocity has done nothing but rise since the end of World War II, and from all indications it will continue to do so).

Such a rule, it is claimed, would eliminate forecasting and lag problems and therefore remove what Friedman sees as the major cause of instability in the economy—the capricious and unpredictable impact of countercyclical monetary policy. As long as the money supply grows at a constant rate each year, be it 3, 4, or 5 percent, any decline into recession will be only temporary. The liquidity provided by a constantly growing money supply will cause aggregate demand to expand. Similarly, if the supply of money does not rise at a more than average rate, any inflationary increase in spending will burn itself out for lack of fuel. Anyway, any discretionary deviations by the central bank would interfere with the natural course of the economy and only make matters worse.

The Joint Economic Committee of Congress has been impressed enough to come part of the way toward a Friedman-type rule, in preference to permitting the Federal Reserve to continue using its own judgment and discretion in the conduct of monetary policy. Quite a few members of the committee are concerned that Federal Reserve "independence" has gone too far. As a means of somewhat reining in the central bank, the committee proposed in 1968 that Congress instruct the Federal Reserve to increase the money supply (demand deposits plus currency) by between 2 and 6 percent annually. Thus far, however, their fellow congressmen have shown no great eagerness to enact the proposal into law.

The Friedman position is based on a number of pillars, each supported by mounds of statistical evidence produced by Friedmanites. However, very little is really known about the length and variability of the time lags. Such evidence as there is, and there is not much, is extremely mixed, as we saw in Chapter 5. Serious research on the subject is only in its early stages, and no consensus is apparent among economists who have worked in the area.

It is ironic—or instructive—that in the final analysis the extremists from both camps, Monetarist and Keynesian, have collectively ganged up on the Federal Reserve. The extreme Monetarists want to shackle it, because their concern with time lags leads them to believe it is both mischievous and harmful. The extreme Keynesians want to subordinate it to fiscal policy, because they think it is either useless or lethal.

In the middle, squabbling but making more common cause than they had thought possible, are the moderates: the moderate Monetarists, who believe that the forecasting-lag problem is not so great as to negate all the potential stabilizing effects of monetary policy; and the moderate Keynesians, who believe that monetary policy probably does change interest rates and/or the availability of credit and that those changes, along with fiscal policy, probably do influence spending decisions in the right way at more or less the right time. While one concentrates mainly on the money supply and the other primarily on credit conditions, they are nevertheless in agreement that some form of countercyclical monetary policy is necessary and, on balance, beneficial.

It seems clear, after all is said and done, that central banking is still at least as much art as science. We simply do not yet know enough to legislate an eternal rule, or even a rule for the next six months, that the Federal Reserve must follow under any and all circumstances. When we do know that much, the Federal Reserve will know it too, and if they are rational men they will follow it regardless of whether it has been enacted into law or not.

Meanwhile, for better or worse, we have no alternative but to rely on our best knowledge and judgment in the formulation of monetary policy. We can only try to make sure that the decision-makers are able and qualified men (or women), with open minds and the capacity to learn from experience.

PART IV
Fiscal Policy

12

FISCAL POLICY VERSUS

MONETARY POLICY

The promoter of a match billed as Fiscal Policy versus Monetary Policy would surely be able to call this encounter the Main Event for the Heavyweight Title. Twenty years ago, however, such a contest would not have made even the preliminaries in the Featherweight division. A forfeit would have been declared in favor of fiscal policy. The reason? It would have been generally believed that monetary policy was unable to defend itself.

The dramatic resurgence of monetary policy since the late 1940s and early 1950s rivals the most classic of comebacks. Two decades ago, monetary policy was relegated to the subservient role of sweeper before the chariot of the Champion. Its functions were to keep bank reserves plentiful and the market for government securities firm, so that interest rates could remain low and nothing impede the right of way of the Great Man. Fiscal policy, alone, in all its Glory, would promote full employment, stabilize prices, ensure economic growth, and eliminate poverty. The reader who thinks that this might be an exaggeration, which it probably is, should reread some of the more exuberant literature typical of that era.

Today they march to a different tune. Although some

die-hard fans of fiscal policy still boo each move of the
monetary authorities, calling every punch a foul and every
feint unfair, their enthusiasm is not what it once was, and
their ranks have dwindled with the passage of time. Government economists now place monetary policy on an
equal footing with fiscal policy in the pursuit of national
economic objectives. Some academic economists even go
so far as to argue that monetary policy should be *the* instrument of economic stabilization, that the impact of fiscal
policy is uncertain, at best. As we indicated earlier, much
of the controversy centers about the debate between the
Monetarists and the Keynesians.

How Fiscal Policy Works

According to the Monetarists, a change in the money supply will alter aggregate spending and GNP by a predictable
amount, since the velocity of money is quite stable. Thus
they contend that monetary policy is a much more effective
instrument than fiscal policy.

Keynesians, on the other hand, are skeptical about the
reliability of the relationship between the money supply
and GNP. As they view it, a change in the money supply
can alter aggregate spending only to the extent that it first
changes interest rates or the availability of credit, and then
only if business or household spending is sensitive to those
changes. There is no direct link between the money supply
and spending. Put briefly, the relationship between the
money supply and GNP is seen as tenuous and variable
since fluctuations in the velocity of money may counteract
changes in its supply.

In Keynesian eyes, changes in government spending or

taxation—the primary tools of fiscal policy—*do* have a direct and fairly predictable impact on GNP. An increase in government spending raises GNP immediately. It also induces additional "multiplier effects" via a GNP-con- sumption-GNP link. As GNP rises because of an initial injection of government expenditure, consumers receive more income; they spend a fraction of this increased in- come, which causes GNP to go up even further. For exam- ple, if government spending rises by $10 billion, income (or GNP) automatically goes up by $10 billion. Of this larger income, consumers will then spend a predictable fraction, say four-fifths, or $8 billion. Since spending by A is income to B, GNP goes up by this $8 billion as well. Of this, consumers then spend another four-fifths, or $6.4 billion. By now, GNP has gone up $24.4 billion. Eventually this process will come to a halt as the successive increments in income and spending become smaller and smaller; but the end result will be an increase in GNP by some multiple of the original increase in government spending.

Changes in tax rates are seen as having a similar multi- ple impact on GNP. If tax rates are lowered, consumers are left with more disposable income. They spend a pre- dictable fraction of this, causing a rise in GNP, which in turn induces additional consumer expenditure. Conclu- sion: to bring about an expansion in spending and GNP, we should increase government spending and/or lower tax rates—that is, create a budget deficit. Anti-inflation policy would call for the opposite: reduce government spending and/or raise tax rates—that is, create a budget surplus.

It is important to note the central role of the GNP- consumption-GNP relationship in the Keynesian "multi- plier" analysis. If consumer spending did not respond to changes in income, tax-rate changes would not affect spending or economic activity, and the "multiplier effects" of changes in government expenditure would be minimal.

Changes in government spending and/or tax rates can be implemented in many different ways. Government spending can be changed via military expenditures, outlays for education, urban renewal, farm price supports, medical research, the space program, or for any other specific government program. Tax receipts can be altered by changing the corporate income tax, the personal income tax, the investment tax credit, or any specific excise or sales tax.

While the impact of a change in any one of these tax or expenditure categories can be made virtually identical with a change in any other one, insofar as the arithmetic effect on GNP is concerned, profound social implications flow from which particular tax or expenditure program is or is not altered. For example, if we are experiencing substantial unemployment and a low rate of economic growth, and fiscal policy is decided upon as the appropriate remedy, a choice arises between lowering taxes and raising government spending. If we lower tax rates, the expansion in GNP will be brought about by private spending. On the other hand, if we increase government spending, this will give us more government services as well as more private purchases. Which alternative we choose should depend on the volume of government (social) services we want.

Going still further: if we decide that we should increase government spending, should it take the form of more money devoted to the space program or an expansion in urban renewal? When we are faced with inflationary pressures, should we cut back military expenditures or anti-poverty programs? These issues are so important that all of Part VI is devoted to them.

Measuring Fiscal Policy

Until now, we have discussed expansionary and contractionary fiscal policy in terms of deficits and surpluses in the
federal budget. A budget deficit is expansionary and a
budget surplus is contractionary. However, just as many
widely used indicators of monetary policy are less than
adequate (see Chapter 9), so there are also serious limitations in using the *current* deficit or surplus as a guide to
the performance of fiscal policy.

The measurement problem stems from the fact that tax
receipts, and hence the size of the deficit or surplus, vary
with GNP. Congress sets tax *rates*, not receipts; receipts
then go up and down with GNP. Given the level of government spending, when GNP rises, tax receipts increase and
surpluses are automatically created (or deficits reduced).
When GNP falls, tax receipts decline and deficits automatically result. Thus, it is impossible to draw any meaningful
conclusions regarding the stance of fiscal policy by comparing a budget surplus in one year, at one level of GNP,
with a deficit in another year, at a different level of GNP.

For example, the existence of a deficit during a recession suggests, at first glance, that fiscal policy is expansionary. It may be, however, that the tax structure is so steep
that it drives income (and thereby tax receipts) down to
recession levels. A deficit may thus actually be the bypro-
duct of a *contractionary* fiscal policy. The tax cut of 1964
was enacted primarily on the basis of such thinking; its
intention was to reduce the "fiscal drag" on the economy.
It was argued that the overly restrictive tax structure—
with taxes rising too rapidly as GNP went up—made it
virtually impossible for GNP to make any sustained headway.

The budget concept that *is* useful as an indicator of the impact of fiscal policy is called the full employment budget. The main problem in comparing deficits or surpluses in year X with year Y is that there are different levels of GNP in the two years. As the diagram indicates, the idea of the full employment budget eliminates this problem. The full employment budget is defined as what the federal budget surplus (or deficit) *would be*, with the expected level of government spending and the existing tax structure, *if the economy were operating at the full employment level of GNP throughout the year*. In this context, a 4 percent unemployment rate is usually considered full employment. This calculated measure, the full employment budget, can be used to evaluate the effects and the performance of fiscal policy more meaningfully than the actual state of the budget, whatever it might be. Indeed, as an indicator of fiscal policy, the full employment budget is a much less ambiguous policy measure than any we thus far have been able to produce for monetary policy.

As an illustration, in 1962, GNP was well below its full employment potential. As the diagram indicates, a low level of GNP produces a poor tax harvest and, consequently, a deficit in the actual budget. Nevertheless, fiscal policy was hardly expansionary. In fact, it was quite the opposite; if GNP had been at the full employment level, or close to it, tax revenues would have risen so greatly that the *full employment budget* would have had a substantial surplus. Conclusion: the fundamental stance of fiscal policy was restrictive, not expansionary, and one reason for the high level of unemployment in 1962 was this impact of fiscal policy—even though the actual budget showed a deficit.

Thus, in a rare example of fiscal bravery, a tax cut was passed by Congress in 1964 despite the existence of a cur-

The Full Employment Budget

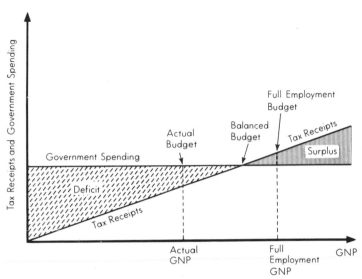

rent budget deficit. A reduction in tax rates swings the tax receipts line (in the diagram) downward and diminishes the full employment surplus. An increase in government spending also shrinks the full employment surplus. A tax-rate increase or a drop in government spending, both of which are restrictive actions, enlarge it. It is clear that changes in the full employment budget reflect basic *discretionary* changes in fiscal policy, as contrasted with movements in the actual budget that can be the passive result of fluctuations in GNP.

Under circumstances such as we had in 1962, if the multiplier effects due to the GNP-consumption-GNP relationship are powerful enough, a tax cut (or an increase in government spending) will eventually succeed in increasing GNP sufficiently to convert an actual deficit into a balanced or even a surplus budget.

This, of course, violates the most sacred canons of "traditional" (or pre-Keynesian) finance. According to the maxims of "orthodox" finance, an actual deficit is a signal to immediately set about balancing the budget by *raising* tax rates and/or *decreasing* government spending—this promptly drives GNP lower, thereby creating an even *larger* deficit, which makes matters worse all around.

Financial Aspects of Fiscal Policy

The fiscal policy mechanism described above is not the whole story. This is recognized by both Keynesians and Monetarists. The total impact on GNP of an expansionary fiscal policy cannot be fully ascertained until the method of financing government deficits is specified. Similarly, the net effect of a reduction in government spending and/or increases in tax rates cannot be fully calculated until the disposition of the surplus is taken into account.

When GNP goes up as the result of deficit spending, the public's need for day-to-day transactions money rises along with it. If the supply of money does not increase simultaneously, the public will find itself short of cash, will presumably sell off some financial assets in order to try to get additional money, and will thereby drive up the rate of interest. This may have an inhibiting effect on private investment spending and on home-building, partly offsetting the expansionary effect of the government's spending.

But a budget deficit can be financed in either of two ways. For one, the government might simply print money to finance itself. Since this is often frowned upon in the best of circles, its twentieth-century equivalent is used instead: the government sells its bonds to the Federal Reserve, which pays for them by creating brand-new checking accounts for the government's use. If this is done, the increased supply of money will probably be sufficient to satisfy the enlarged need for money and interest rates will not rise. In this case, there will be little or no offset to the expansionary impact of the deficit spending, and GNP will be able to rise without interference from the monetary side.

Alternatively, the deficit might be financed by the sale of government securities to the public. (Buy Government Bonds and Help Defend Democracy!) If this is done, however, the pressure on financial markets is actually intensified, since the increase in the supply of new bonds on the market drives up the rate of interest even further. Decreased investment spending will offset an even larger portion of the increased government spending. The net effect, according to the Keynesians, is still expansionary, although less so than in the case of money-financed deficits.

In any event, regardless of details, the important point is that the execution of fiscal policy is inextricably mixed up with monetary implications. The two cannot be separated.

The Monetarists versus the Keynesians

The Keynesian position is that any fiscal action, no matter how it is financed, will have a significant impact on GNP. Keynesians do not deny that interest rates are likely to rise as GNP goes up, unless new money is forthcoming to meet cash needs for day-to-day transactions. Thus, they admit that a deficit financed by money creation is more expansionary than one financed by bond sales to the public, and that both are more expansionary than increased government spending financed by taxation. However, Keynesians do not believe that the decrease in private investment spending caused by higher interest rates will be great enough to offset fully the government's fiscal actions. They think that the net effect will be significant, and in the right direction, regardless of what financing methods are used.

One reason for this conclusion is that higher interest rates themselves are seen as having dual effects. They may reduce private investment spending, but they may also lead people to economize on their cash balances, thereby supplying part of the need for new transactions money from formerly idle cash holdings. Put somewhat differently, even if a deficit is not financed by new money, the velocity of existing money will accelerate (in response to higher interest rates) so that the old money supply combined with the new velocity will be able to support a higher level of spending and GNP.

The Monetarist view, on the other hand, is that unless a budget deficit is financed by new money creation it will not alter GNP. Since velocity is seen as more or less constant, a direct link exists between the money supply and GNP. In order for GNP to rise, the money supply must expand.

If a fiscal deficit is financed by printing money, it will indeed increase spending and GNP. But according to the Monetarists, it is not the deficit that is responsible—it is the additional money. Furthermore, a deficit is a very clumsy way to go about increasing the money supply. Why not simply have the Federal Reserve engage in open market operations? That would accomplish the same purpose, a change in the money supply, without getting involved in budget deficits or surpluses.

As the Monetarists see it, a fiscal deficit financed in any other way—as by selling bonds to the public—will not affect aggregate GNP. True, the government will be spending more. But others will wind up spending less. Net result: no change in total spending or in GNP. The rise in government spending will *initially* increase GNP. However, this will increase the demand for cash for transactions purposes and drive interest rates up, and bond sales to finance the government's expenditures will drive rates up still further. The public will be buying government bonds and financing the government, instead of buying corporate bonds and financing business firms. The rise in interest rates will reduce private investment spending by as much as government spending is increased, and that will be the end of the story. Government fiscal policy, unaccompanied by changes in the supply of money, merely changes the proportion of government spending relative to private spending.

Anti-inflationary fiscal policy encounters similar objections from the Monetarists. An increase in tax rates that generates a fiscal surplus reduces private income and consumer spending. If the government destroys or simply holds the money, the tax revenue it has collected over and above its expenditures, then the surplus is accompanied by a reduction of the money supply in private pockets. Both Keynesians and Monetarists would agree that this is anti-inflationary, although for different reasons—the Keynesians because of the direct fiscal impact on consumer spending, with the tax increase reducing people's take-home pay, and the Monetarists because of the contraction in the money supply.

But if the government uses the surplus to retire part of the national debt, the funds flow back into the economy. The government retires debt by buying back its bonds. Bond prices are driven up, interest rates fall, and private investment spending increases. Keynesians would argue that GNP will still decline, that the debt retirement is a minor ripple on a huge wave. Monetarists, however, would say that private investment spending will increase until it replaces the cutback in consumer spending, leaving no net effect whatsoever on GNP.

As we stressed in Chapter 4, the fight between fiscal and monetary policy can be decided only by resort to empirical evidence. The Keynesians claim that the power of fiscal policy was demonstrated by the success of the 1964 tax cut in bringing the economy up to a high level of employment. The Monetarists contend that fiscal policy alone is useless and that it was the rapid expansion of the money supply during the months preceding the tax cut that did the job. They also point to the failure of the 1968 tax surcharge to stop inflation. The Keynesians respond by asserting that acceleration of the war in Vietnam undid the impact of the 1968 tax increase.

Frustrated, let us turn to the Federal Reserve–MIT– Penn econometric model that we dissected in Chapter 5. Unfortunately, it is also ambiguous. An increase of $1 billion in the money supply raises GNP by $2.5 billion after one year, according to the model, while a $1 billion increase in government spending raises GNP by about $3 billion over the same time interval. After three years, however, their relative effectiveness is reversed: the impact of fiscal policy is no greater than after one year, while monetary policy gathers momentum and becomes considerably more powerful in the second and third years.

The Monetarist model of the Federal Reserve Bank of St. Louis is less wishy-washy than its FMP sparring partner: an increase of $1 billion in the money supply raises GNP by over $5 billion after one year, while a similar increase in government spending has zero impact on GNP

How To Score

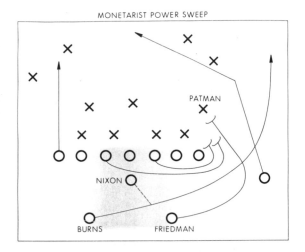

Dick (the scrambler) Nixon hands off to Doc Burns—who streaks down the right sideline behind a big block (actually a clip) by Uncle Milty Friedman that completely upends A. (for Always) Wright Patman.

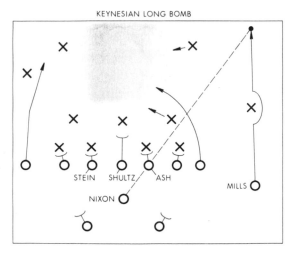

Dick Nixon hits Wee Willie Mills with a TD pass (as Howard Cosell goes wild in the booth)—fantastic blocking by the unsung heroes of the front line, led by George Shultz, Herbie Stein, and Roy Ash.

over the same time period. An increase in government spending raises GNP after six months, but by the time a year has elapsed other types of spending have declined to offset the expansion in government expenditures. What other types of spending? On this the St. Louis model is silent, just as it is silent on the transmission mechanism through which money affects spending. Indeed, it is this agnosticism on the transmission process and the surprising result with respect to fiscal policy that make the St. Louis model so incomprehensible to many Keynesians.

Who gets the verdict has implications far beyond flattering the egos of economists with vested intellectual interests on opposite sides of the fence. If we are in a recession and use easy money to raise GNP, interest rates will fall and private investment and home-building will expand. On the other hand, if we use fiscal policy—lowering tax rates or increasing government spending—consumer spending or social services will be favored instead.

If we are in a boom and want to reduce aggregate spending, tight money will hit housing hard; tight fiscal policy probably will not. If a vibrant housing industry is important for national social and economic welfare—on the theory that the American Dream consists of each citizen owning his own home with a well in the backyard— perhaps we should rely mainly on easy money to stop recessions and mainly on tight fiscal policy to halt inflation.

A rational overall stabilization policy would evaluate all of these elements, and more, before embarking on a course of action. There are likely to be other side effects, some desirable, others undesirable. Often political considerations will be involved as well. It is difficult, for example, to raise taxes in an election year. Not to mention the influence that various pressure groups, both business and labor, are likely to bring to bear on such decisions.

In any case, the importance of *both* fiscal and monetary policy, and the numerous interrelations between them, makes it plain that there can be no clear-cut winner. If either fiscal policy or monetary policy is declared the victor, to the neglect and subjugation of the other, it is we who will be the losers.

PART V

Of Bonds, Stocks, and Intermediaries

13

SHOULD WE WORRY ABOUT THE

NATIONAL DEBT?

"Personally," said President Eisenhower, in his State of the Union Message in 1960, "I do not feel that any amount can properly be called a surplus as long as the nation is in debt. I prefer to think of such an item as a reduction in our children's inherited mortgage."

In the same vein, Senator Harry F. Byrd, Sr., pondered the $275 billion national debt in 1955 and gloomily predicted: "The debt today is the debt incurred by this generation, but tomorrow it will be debt on our children and grandchildren, and it will be for them to pay, both principal and interest."

Debt worriers are fond of statistical computations. We now have a national debt of some $440 billion (in the form of marketable and nonmarketable government securities, held by the public and by government agencies) and a population of 210 million. Conclusion: every man, woman, and child in this country owes about $2,100, whether he knows it or not. Every newborn infant starts life not only with a pat on the back but also with a $2,100 share of the national debt hanging over his head.

Agonizing over the size of the public debt is one of our major national preoccupations. As the National Worry

Meter indicates, the most recent scientific poll of a stratified sample of our population, taken personally by the authors during spring vacation, showed that The National Debt ranks close to the top of all our worries. It is considered more worrisome than either The Mafia or Communism, although it is still viewed as somewhat less of a problem than the Worst Thing we have to contend with, The Younger Generation.

Is the situation really all that bad? Are the debt worriers right when they warn us that, by passing on a national debt of $440 billion, we are burdening future generations with a weight it will be almost impossible for them to bear? Are they correct in cautioning us, with stern voices, that we are penalizing those as yet unborn by forcing them to pay for our own vices and follies?

The National Debt Equals the National Credit

The national debt is essentially the net result of past and present fiscal policy, mostly past. It is the sum of all past deficits, less surpluses, in the federal budget. A budget deficit requires that the government either print money or borrow to cover the deficit, and most modern governments choose to borrow (that is, sell government securities). As a result, we acquire a national debt, embodied in the form of government bonds; the total of government securities outstanding *is* the national debt. It is increased by every additional deficit we incur and finance by issuing more bonds.

If it is a debt, we must owe it to someone. Indeed we do—we owe it mostly to ourselves. Most of our government's bonds are internally held, that is, they are owned

The National Worry Meter

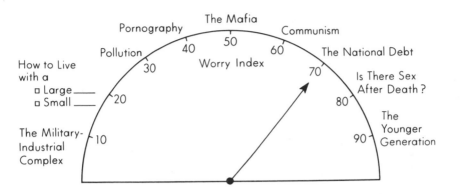

by citizens of the United States. Thus, while we the people (as the United States) *owe* $440 billion, we the people (as owners of government securities) are simultaneously *owed* close to the same amount. A government bond is, after all, an asset for whoever buys it.

All evidences of debt must appear on *two* balance sheets, and government securities are no different from any other IOU in this respect. Every IOU appears on the balance sheet of the debtor, as a liability; but it also turns up, not surprisingly, on the balance sheet of whoever is holding it, its owner, this time as an *asset*. Thus, every liability necessarily implies the existence of a financial asset owned by someone else. For the same reason, every *financial* asset implies a corresponding liability on the part of someone else.

This accounting fact of life has interesting ramifications. It means, for one, that merely creating money cannot, in and of itself, make a country richer, a conclusion that always pleases conservatives. For after all, money is a financial asset, which implies that somewhere else there is a corresponding liability. If liabilities go up as rapidly as assets, the country as a whole (including both the government and the private sector) can be getting no richer.

Most of our money is in the form of demand deposits, which are liabilities of commerical banks. The part of our money that is in the form of coin or currency is a liability of either the United States Treasury or the Federal Reserve, depending on which agency issued it.

Thus merely creating money can hardly make a nation richer, no matter how much it creates. To become richer— to increase its net worth—a country must increase its output of *real* assets, its production of real goods and services. As conservatives like to point out, if we want to become wealthier, we must work harder and produce more. Printing money, per se, will not do it.

By the same token, however, exactly the same logic also implies that one of the conservatives' favorite incantations is equally false: namely, the belief that increasing the national debt makes a country poorer. Government bonds are liabilities to the government but are financial assets to whoever owns them. If the national debt increases, someone's financial assets go up as much as the government's liabilities. If domestically held assets rise along with liabilities, the country as a whole can be getting no poorer.

The very term *national debt* is thus a half-truth. If it is a domestically held debt, it could just as well be called the *national credit*. Both labels are half-truths. As with all liabilities, it is *both* a debt (to the borrower) *and* a credit (to the lender).

To become poorer—to reduce its net worth—a country must reduce its holdings of real assets, curtail its production of *real* goods and services. Increasing the national debt, no matter how high, cannot in and of itself make a country poorer so long as it is owned internally. (Actually, about $50 billion of our $440 billion national debt is held by foreign citizens and institutions.)

Nor does an increasing national debt, just because of its size, impose a burden on future generations. As long as the debt is held internally, neither the interest nor the principal represents a dead weight on the backs of our children and grandchildren. The taxes that must be raised to pay the interest are merely transfers from one group within the economy, the taxpayers, to another group, the bondholders. Future generations inherit tax liabilities, but they also inherit bonds and the right to receive the interest on them.

Even if the debt had to be paid off, future generations, as inheritors of the bonds, would be making payments of the principal to themselves. In fact, of course, the federal debt never has to be fully repaid any more than does the debt of any going concern, public or private. As parts of the debt come due, they can be repaid with fresh borrowings. Continuous refinancing is typical of the modern successful corporation, because confidence in the company's ability to earn future income makes holding its bonds both safe and profitable. Similarly, confidence in the continuing viability and taxing power of the federal government eliminates the need for net repayment of principal, either currently or in the future.

The Real Burden of the Debt: I

Does this mean, then, that the debt worriers are completely off the track? Not quite, and therein lies the story of the *real* burden of the debt as contrasted with the imaginary burden.

In the first place, holdings of government bonds are not

evenly distributed among the population. Some of us have more than our $2,100 share, much more; and some have less, much less. Thus current interest payments on the debt, while "only" an internal transfer from taxpayers to bondholders, may create problems of legitimate concern to the public. If taxpayers are largely from the lower and middle income groups, while bondholders are primarily in the upper income brackets, then the tax collection → interest payment transfer will increase the inequality of income distribution. Little is known about the pattern of interest payments on the government debt according to income of the recipient. This transfer *may*, therefore, interfere with social objectives of reducing income inequality.

Furthermore, if the federal debt grows at a faster rate than GNP, tax rates may have to be increased in order to meet interest payments. Higher tax rates may reduce work incentives. If so, production falls and overall economic well-being decreases. In the United States, however, the national debt has actually declined, quite substantially, as a proportion of our gross national product. In 1945, the national debt was about 130 percent of GNP; in 1955, 70 percent; and in 1965, 45 percent. Today, it is slightly less than 40 percent of GNP.

Even if the debt falls as a proportion of GNP, if interest *rates* go up sufficiently then tax rates may have to be raised to meet the interest payments, thus again possibly reducing work incentives. Interest rates have indeed risen since 1945, but nevertheless the interest "burden"—interest charges as a proportion of GNP—has not increased. Over the past twenty-five years, annual interest payments have been stable at between 1½ and 2 percent of GNP.

The Real Burden of the Debt: II

Aside from the possible income-redistribution and work-incentive problems associated with interest payments on the national debt, there is one way in which the debt might impose a burden, a cost, on future generations. This involves not the interest, but the principal itself.

As we noted above, a country will become poorer only if it reduces its output of real assets, its ability to produce real goods and services. In this sense, a very meaningful sense, the wealth of future generations can be measured by the real capital stock they inherit, the real productive capacity of the economy we bequeath to them. A smaller capital stock permits less production, hence less consumption. A larger capital stock enables the economy to produce more, hence consume more.

Assume that the economy is already operating at a full capacity rate of production and that the budget is balanced. Whereupon the government increases its spending, financing its additional expenditures by sufficient new *taxation* to forestall inflation. In this case, the increased use of resources by the government comes primarily at the expense of consumption. Consumers, left with less after-tax income, have to cut back their spending by as much as government spending has been stepped up.

Alternatively, under the same initial circumstances, assume that the additional government spending is *debt-financed* rather than tax-financed, and that a tight monetary policy is used along with debt-financing to prevent inflation. Now interest rates will rise and the increased use of resources by the government will come primarily at the expense of investment instead of consumption. The higher interest rates will release resources from private investment for use by the government, with investment spending cut back by as much as government spending has been increased.

As a result, the building of new plants and equipment will be curtailed, and future generations will consequently inherit a smaller capital stock. Future productive capacity is lower than it might have been. In this limited sense, the "burden" of debt-financed current government expenditure is transferred to future generations.

Two qualifications are necessary. First, note that the argument assumes we start initially from a full capacity rate of production, roughly a full employment level of GNP. If the additional government spending were to take place during a recession, when there are idle resources available, then there would be no "burden" on future generations, no matter how it was financed. During a recession there are unemployed resources that can be tapped, so the government can increase its spending without anyone else reducing his. There would be no reason to permit a rise in interest rates, since the danger of inflation would be minimal, and an expansion in spending and GNP would be beneficial to all.

Under such circumstances, the future capital stock is not diminished. In fact, if the government's deficit spending succeeds in getting us out of the recession, the future capital stock will probably be *enlarged*. Thus increasing the national debt during a recession, instead of imposing a burden on future generations, is actually doing them a favor.

Second, the "burden" argument totally ignores what the government spends the money on. Assuming full employment, if the government's expenditure is for current consumption purposes—such as subsidizing inexpensive lunches for congressmen or schoolchildren—then total capital passed on to the future is indeed reduced. But if the government builds highways, dams, or increases any type of capital asset that raises future productivity, the increased investment by the government replaces the decreased investment by private business. Future generations will inherit the same capital stock, except more will be in the form of public capital and less in the form of private capital.

Moving from theory to reality, the fact of the matter is that about 50 percent of our public debt stems directly from World War II military spending. In 1941 our national debt was $65 billion, and in 1945 it was $280 billion. Most of these expenditures occurred during a period of full employment. Yet few would call this a burden passed on to the future. Without it, we might well have had no future.

The Nuts and Bolts of Debt Management

Given a national debt of $440 billion, its day-to-day management has implications for the functioning of financial markets and for economic stability. How can the debt be refinanced most smoothly when portions of it come due? How much of the debt should be in the form of short-term Treasury bills, how much in the form of long-term Treasury bonds?

The dimensions of the Treasury's debt-management chore can best be appreciated by realizing that about $135 billion of the debt comes due every year and must be paid off. How? By refinancing it, of course—that is, by borrowing $135 billion from someone else. The Treasury can replace the maturing issues with new short-term Treasury bills, or with intermediate- or long-term bonds, thus providing some elbow room for altering the maturity structure of the debt.

In many respects, debt management is a close relative of open market operations. The effects are very much the same, for example, whether the Federal Reserve sells Treasury bills (which we call open market operations) or whether the United States Treasury sells them (which we call debt management).

What are the objectives of day-to-day debt management? One goal is to minimize the interest cost of the debt to the taxpayers. But this can hardly be the only objective. If it were, the Treasury could minimize the interest cost— indeed, reduce it to zero—by simply printing money and buying back all the outstanding securities. That is, it could replace its interest-bearing debt (bills and bonds) with its non-interest-bearing debt (money). Obviously, the Treasury does not "monetize the debt," because to do so would probably result in massive inflation, and the Treasury also has the objective of managing the debt to promote economic stability.

These two objectives often dictate opposite policy actions. Minimizing the interest cost suggests that when we are in a recession, and interest rates are low across the board, the Treasury should refund its maturing issues with new long-term bonds, thus ensuring low interest payments for itself well into the future. During boom periods, on the other hand, when interest rates are typically high, the Treasury should refinance by selling short-term issues, Treasury bills, so the government does not have to continue paying high rates after yields have fallen to more normal levels.

Stabilization objectives call for just the opposite policies. When we are in a recession, the last thing we want to do is to raise long-term interest rates, which is precisely what pushing long-term securities onto the market would accomplish. During boom periods, when we *do* want to raise long rates, is when we should sell long-term bonds.

Thus the objective of minimizing interest costs dictates lengthening the maturity structure of the debt (more long-term bonds relative to short-term bills) during recession periods and shortening the maturity structure during boom periods. Whereas for purposes of economic stabilization we should try to shorten the maturity structure during recessions and to lengthen it during prosperity.

A complication that makes it difficult to lengthen the maturity structure of the federal debt, especially during prosperity periods, is the archaic 4¼ percent legal ceiling on government bond interest rates. By virtue of a law passed in 1917, the Treasury is not allowed to pay more than a 4¼ percent interest rate on bonds with seven or more years to maturity. Since long-term market interest rates have generally been well above 4¼ percent in recent years, the Treasury has been unable to offer competitive yields on long-term securities and thus has had no choice but to borrow via shorter-maturity issues. (In a daring break with tradition, Congress has recently grabbed the bull by the tail and looked the situation squarely in the eye; it has modified the law to enable the Treasury to issue up to $10 billion of bonds at rates above 4¼ percent.)

One technique of debt-lengthening is known as advance refunding. The Treasury offers the holders of a selected security issue, which still has a number of years to maturity, the opportunity to exchange their securities for a new issue with a longer maturity. The investor receives a new security with a slightly higher yield without having to realize a capital gain or loss on his old security. This method facilitates debt-lengthening by isolating the likely purchasers of long-term issues without the Treasury's having to resort to the open market. However, despite Congress's derring-do, the 4¼ percent statutory interest rate ceiling has severely inhibited the utilization of this technique.

Debt-management policy must be administered in coordination with monetary and fiscal policy. If minimizing the interest cost is the primary goal of the Treasury, then monetary and fiscal policy will have to take appropriate action to offset this counterstabilization debt policy. If economic stabilization is the primary objective of debt management, then the monetary and fiscal authorities can take this into account and reduce the forcefulness of their own actions.

Coordination between the monetary and debt-management authorities is also essential on a continuing basis because of the vast magnitude of the Treasury's frequent refunding operations. When the Treasury refinances maturing securities, the dollar amount involved is often so large that it needs help from the central bank. If the Federal Reserve is pursuing a tight money policy, for example, it will often become less aggressive and resort to a policy of keeping an "even keel" in the money markets as the date of a refinancing approaches. In effect, the central bank will mark time for a few weeks so that orderly money-market conditions prevail while the Treasury goes through the mechanics of the refunding operation. It is difficult enough for the Treasury to roll over so much debt without being forced to cope with additional complications resulting from actions of the monetary authorities.

Monetary policy, fiscal policy, and debt management are often considered the three primary tools of stabilization* policy. In practice, however, debt management has typically been the runt of the litter. Perhaps that is just as well. Given the power of monetary and fiscal policy to implement national economic goals, perhaps debt management can make its most significant contribution by successfully accomplishing the more limited but not unimportant task of continuously refinancing a very large volume of securities without unduly disturbing the nation's financial markets.

14

DOES MONETARY POLICY

AFFECT THE STOCK MARKET?

Any civic or social club program chairman knows that if he announces that next week's meeting will feature a renowned speaker on "The Crisis in America's Cities," hardly anyone will show up. But if he announces that the topic will be "The Outlook for the Stock Market" and mentions a speaker no one ever heard of, the hall will be packed. It would be hard to find a subject that intrigues people more than the stock market. Everyone knows about stocks: how they always go up, and how they can make you rich. Forty years ago everyone knew about stocks: how they always go down, and how they can make you destitute.

Why do stock prices go up and down? Not so much particular stocks, like IBM or Xerox, but why does the entire stock market soar or shudder, with all stocks more or less rising or falling together?

It is a fact of life that the total supply of stocks in existence is more or less fixed. What changes is not so much the number of shares lying around—in vaults, under mattresses, and concealed between the pages of the family Bible—but the price of each.

For example, the market value of all the publicy held shares of stock now in existence amounts to something like

$1,200 billion. Ten years ago it was about $600 billion, and ten years before that about $200 billion. And yet in the past twenty years corporations have raised relatively little money by issuing new stock, perhaps $70 or $75 billion at most. This means, and the word has obviously gotten around, that almost all of that $1,200 billion—probably at least $1,100 billion of it—represents price appreciation of existing shares.

The fact that the total supply outstanding is relatively fixed does not, of course, imply that the amount offered on the market need be fixed. People who have bought, and even some who haven't, can always sell. Thus in recent years stocks have been drifting out of the hands of individual investors, who have been selling on balance, into the plush suites of institutional investors, who have been buying. A decade ago pension funds, mutual funds, insurance companies, and other institutional investors held about 20 percent of the market value of outstanding shares; now they hold about 30 percent. But 70 percent or $840 billion is still held by individuals, about 35 million of them, and each and every one is out to make a killing.

Strangely enough, given the widespread interest in the stock market, economists have generally had very little to say about it. The most popular postwar college textbook, Paul Samuelson's *Economics*, is estimated to have sold over two and a half million copies since it first appeared in 1948. Considering the royalties accruing to so popular an author, and a leading economist in the bargain, one would think he might have accumulated both the wherewithal and the trained experience to discover at long last the secret of what makes the market tic. But if Paul has found out, he isn't telling! The latest edition of *Economics* contains only 5 pages on the stock market (out of 868).

Some economists are less reticent than Professor Samuelson about letting us in on why stock prices fluctuate. Their explanations have ranged from the influence of sunspots on men's emotional behavior to the conspiratorial machinations of shadowy figures in high places. However, the explanations that are of most interest to us here deal with money and monetary policy.

Is it true, as some claim, that the elusive clue to movements in overall stock prices is to be found in changes in the money supply? Or does the secret lie, as others believe, in changes in monetary policy in general? If the former are correct, and to some extent the latter, perhaps all the paraphernalia that market analysts now so laboriously wrestle with for signs of the future can be put aside; the best tout sheet might turn out to be the weekly Federal Reserve statement.

A Money Supply View of Stock Prices

The belief that fluctuations in the money supply provide the key to movements in stock prices is based on a logical series of cause-and-effect hypotheses that contain elements of both Monetarist and Keynesian thinking. In its simplest form, the reasoning is as follows: when the Federal Reserve increases the money supply at a faster than normal rate, the public, finding itself with more cash than it needs for current transactions purposes, spends some of its excess money buying financial assets, including stocks. Since the supply of stocks is more or less fixed, especially in the short run, this incremental demand raises their price. Some stocks will go up more than others, and some may go down, depending on the prospects for particular companies, but overall the average of stock prices will rise.

Or the transmission process might be somewhat more

complex, but with similar results. The increase in the money supply may first lead the public to step up its *bond* purchases, thereby raising bond prices. Higher bond prices imply lower interest rates. With bonds yielding less, some potential bond purchasers are likely to switch over to the now relatively more attractive stock market. The demand for stocks expands because their substitute, bonds, has become more expensive, just as the demand for Yamahas (the 650s) will expand when their alternative, Hondas (the 750s), become more expensive. (Not to mention the Suzuki.)

In either case, the result is the same. Whether the chain of causation is direct, from the money supply to stock prices, or indirect, through the bond market and interest rates, an increase in the money supply accelerates the demand for stocks and thereby leads to higher stock prices.

Conversely, decreases in the money supply—or increases at a slower rate than necessary to provide for the transactions needs of a growing economy—leave the public with shortages of funds. Result: among other things, a cutback in stock purchases—again, either directly or because, with higher interest rates, bonds become more attractive buys. This reduced demand for stocks lowers their prices.

Conclusion: a rapidly expanding money supply leads to higher stock values; inadequate monetary growth leads to a bear market. Nevertheless, persuasive as the underlying reasoning may seem, all too frequently the facts simply do not bear it out. Evidently, too many other crosscurrents simultaneously impinge on the stock market, such as business expectations and political developments. Like so many other single-cause explanations in economics, this simplified view of stock price determination contains too much truth to ignore but not enough to make it very reliable in the clutch.

Consider 1929, and the couple of years before and after. From mid-1927 to mid-1928, the money supply increased by 1.6 percent; from mid-1928 to mid-1929, it increased by 1.2 percent. The stock market, meanwhile, going its merry way, *doubled.*

In the next two years, from mid-1929 to mid-1931, the money supply contracted by about 5 percent each year. If the stock market was merely reacting to changes in the money supply, it was by all odds the biggest overreaction in history, because the proverbial bottom dropped out and the market promptly lost all the gains it had made in the previous two years and then some. Compared with *that* kind of overreaction, Mayor Daley's minions appear more wishy-washy than Charlie Brown.

Furthermore, it is not at all clear precisely what is cause and what is effect. Did the market crash because, among other things, the money supply contracted? Or did the money supply contract because the market crashed (as banks called speculative margin loans and demand deposits were wiped off the books)? The latter explanation is as logical as the former.

The 1929 market collapse, as many see it, was due to a number of interrelated factors: an unwarranted mood of euphoric optimism prior to the crash, excessive speculative activity, fundamental weakness in underlying business conditions, and so on. The money supply, if it influenced the break at all, did so only as one among many causes.

None of which is meant to imply that the money supply was or is unimportant. If it had been rapidly and forcefully restored to its 1929 level by 1930, or even 1931, the depression that was initiated by the stock market collapse would probably not have been either as severe or as long as it turned out to be. That the Federal Reserve stood by, wringing its hands, while the money supply declined by

30 percent from 1929 to 1933, undoubtedly intensified and prolonged what we now call the Great Depression. But that is a very different thing from saying that movements in the money supply caused or could have given one even a vague idea of the heights or the depths to which stock prices went from 1927 to 1931. As a matter of fact, most of the drop in the money supply occurred *after* 1931; by that time, however, the market was too weary to do any reacting, either over or under.

To come closer to the present, in 1940 the stock market fell 15 percent even though the money supply was then rising 15 percent (on top of a similar rise the year before). In 1962, again, the market tumbled despite an increasing money supply.

On other not infrequent occasions, however, it is true that declines in stock prices *were* preceded or accompanied by declines in the money supply, as in 1957, 1960 and 1969. And often increases in stock prices were indeed associated with increases in the money supply, as in 1967 and 1968.

In at least some of these instances, however, both stock prices and the money supply might conceivably have been reacting to a third causal force, perhaps an upturn in business conditions stimulated by the outbreak of war ( ) peace ( )—check one—a spurt in consumer spending, or something else. An improvement in business conditions, regardless of cause, typically leads to an expansion in bank business loans, and to a larger money supply; and to brighter profit prospects, and thereby higher stock prices. As the history of business cycles indicates, such upswings (or downturns) are capable of generating a cumulative push that can work up considerable momentum, carrying *both* the money supply and stock prices along with it.

The accompanying chart provides some idea of the pitfalls involved in reading a cause-and-effect relationship into two sets of statistics simply because they move together. The heavy line indicates the movement of stock prices, annually, from the end of 1960 through the end of 1966, using stock prices at the end of 1960 as the base (= 100).

The thin dashed line, on a similar index basis, is the movement of the money supply annually, also from the end of 1960 through the end of 1966. Over this particular six-year period, changes in the money supply clearly bore little relationship to turning points in stock prices.

Finally, the chart also includes a third line (W). Its

Stock Prices and Other Variables, 1960-66

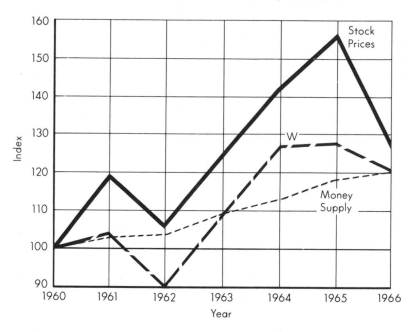

Stock Prices = Dow-Jones Industrials, monthly closing averages for December of each year (December 1960 = 100).
Money Supply = Demand deposits plus currency, monthly averages for December of each year (December 1960 = 100).

movements are obviously closely related to changes in stock prices. Almost without exception, the line labeled W and the line tracing stock prices move up and down together.

Cause and effect? The line labeled W, make of it what you will, is an annual index (1960 = 100) of the number of times members of the old Washington Senators baseball team struck out, each year, over the period 1960 through 1966. (Source: The Sporting News's *Official Baseball Guide and Record Book*, Annual, 1960–66.) For at least these years, evidently, an investor trying to forecast turning points in the stock market would have been better off spending his time reading the box scores instead of the money supply figures.

However, upon reflection, perhaps this is no accidental relationship, after all. Might it be statistical confirmation of the popular suspicion, heretofore unproven, that the affluent modern ballplayer pays more attention to his investments than to his batting average?

Monetary Policy and Wall Street

Once we expand our horizon to encompass more than the money supply alone, there seems to be agreement that monetary policy, in general, frequently does have a considerable influence on the stock market. The consensus appears to be that it is by no means the only influence, and often is far overshadowed by other forces and events; nevertheless, it is widely believed that on balance monetary policy has had a substantial effect on stock prices at times in the past, *especially the recent past*, and is likely to continue to do so in the foreseeable future.

This is quite aside from the power the Federal Reserve has to set margin requirements on stock purchases. In an attempt to prevent a repetition of the speculative wave, financed heavily with borrowed funds, that had carried the market to dizzy heights in 1928 and until the Fall of 1929, Congress in the 1930s authorized the Federal Reserve to impose margin (or minimum downpayment) requirements on the purchase of stocks. If the margin requirement is 100 percent, then 100 percent cash must be put up and no borrowing at all is permitted. If the margin requirement is 80 percent, that much of one's own cash must be put up when buying a security, and only the remaining 20 percent can be financed by borrowing from a bank or a broker. Of course, you could always finance the entire amount by borrowing from your brother-in-law and no one would be the wiser (except perhaps, in the long run, your brother-in-law).

High margin requirements probably have helped restrain speculation in stocks, particularly by those who could least afford it. Nevertheless, if the Federal Reserve had only this device to influence the market, it would be relying on a weak reed indeed. Margin requirements are 100 percent at Santa Anita and Hialeah, but, at last report, speculative activity by those who could not afford it as well as by those who could appeared to be unimpaired.

The impact of overall monetary policy on stock prices stems not so much from the Federal Reserve's power to set margin requirements as from its influence over the money supply, the entire spectrum of interest rates and financial markets, and current and expected business conditions. Surprisingly, perhaps, it is in the recent past, rather than ten, twenty, or thirty years ago, that the effects of monetary policy on stock prices are most clearly visible. The credit squeezes of 1966 and 1969 are prime examples.

During 1966, for instance, the money supply increased at a slower than normal rate. Bankers, businessmen, and the general public, carried away by the skyrocketing interest rates, labeled the episode the Great Credit Crunch of 1966. Credit availability was sharply curtailed and interest rates on fixed-income securities soared. Stock prices tumbled about 20 percent during the first ten months of the year, despite continued inflation and booming business conditions—a rather clear indication of the potency of tight money, when applied vigorously, in affecting stock prices.

The easy money policy that prevailed during 1967 and most of 1968 was correspondingly accompanied by a rapid and lengthy upturn in the stock market. The subsequent reimposition of exceedingly tight money in 1969, however, was followed by a prompt collapse of stock prices. The Dow-Jones industrial average plunged from 985 in late 1968 to the 630 level in mid-1970, when it finally began to turn around.

During the three decades from the early 1930s to the early 1960s, the reaction of the stock market to monetary policy was less prompt and less predictable than it has recently been. During those years, stocks frequently seemed to go their own way, regardless of what the central bank was doing. Not so any more; since the mid-1960s, there appears to be a rather clear cause-and-effect relationship between the general stance of monetary policy and movements in stock prices.

There are two reasons for this change. First, the central bank has recently been acting with more authority than it did previously. In retrospect, during the 1950s and early 1960s, when the Federal Reserve was just testing the air once again after almost twenty years of virtual hibernation, a wiggle in long-term bond rates would cause it to beat a hasty retreat. It was afraid to probe too far for fear of starting a recession. An increase in interest rates on long-term government bonds from 3½ to 4 percent was considered a hazardous venture.

The credit crunch of 1966, however, gave the monetary authorities a different perspective. Prices fell on long-term government bonds to the point where effective interest rates approached 5 percent—not so high by later standards, but the equivalent of Mount Everest then—and yields on some intermediate-term Treasury bonds went over 6 percent. The economy thrashed and strained, but it did not collapse. It proved to be more resilient than many had supposed.

However, something else did happen. For the first time in a generation, many investors became aware that such things as bonds existed. And that, under certain conditions, they were more attractive additions to one's portfolio than stocks. The rise in bond interest rates (which means a fall in bond prices) thus had repercussions in the stock market; some individual and institutional investors held off buying stocks, or sold some they had, and bought bonds instead, thereby driving stock prices down as well.

In theory, the prices of stocks and bonds *should* move together in precisely that way, since they are substitutes for each other in investor portfolios just as Yamahas and Hondas are on the highway (with or without monkey bars and sissy bars). As we noted earlier in this chapter, if the price of bonds falls (implying higher interest rates), some buyers should switch out of stocks and into the now relatively more attractive bonds—thus causing the price of stocks to fall too. For similar reasons, if the price of bonds rises, stock prices should rise also.

However, during the 1950s, this relationship did not hold very closely. For most of that decade, interest rates on bonds were slowly rising, cautiously adjusting upward from artificially low war and postwar levels. Slowly rising bond interest rates imply slowly falling bond prices. Stock prices, on the other hand, were ebullient during most of the decade.

With yields on bonds and stocks now at more realistic levels relative to each other, the sympathetic relationship between the two has reasserted itself and is apt to continue into the future. From now on, when the Federal Reserve bangs bonds around, stocks are likely to get a nosebleed.

The second reason why monetary policy affects stock prices more today than ten or twenty years ago is simply that the Federal Reserve has made believers out of many former skeptics. If the Federal Reserve is ineffectual, who cares? But if monetary policy is effective in influencing the course of the economy, then a lot of people care a great deal. Today, many more financial analysts and observers of economic trends are persuaded that the central bank is able to achieve its announced objectives, or at least come reasonaby close, than thought so a decade or two back.

Since stock prices presumably reflect views of future business conditions, if the Federal Reserve is believed to have an impact on the economy then what the Federal Reserve does will have an impact on the stock market. What really matters, of course, when it comes to the stock market, is not so much whether monetary policy actually is effective, but whether people think it is. Only a few think the monetary authorities are all-powerful, but many are convinced they are potent enough to worry about.

15

WHAT IS FINANCIAL

INTERMEDIATION?

Financial intermediation played an important role, it is said, in permitting monetary velocity to rise during the 1950s. Financial *dis*intermediation, on the other hand, was a significant factor in aggravating the extremely tight monetary conditions of 1966 and 1969. The words are big, but the process, it turns out, is commonplace and familiar. It is so ordinary, in fact, that we can add to those who have been talking prose all their lives, and were not aware of it, the millions who have been engaged in some aspect of financial intermediation or disintermediation, and did not realize it.

Financial intermediaries are nothing more than financial institutions—such as commercial and savings banks, savings and loan associations, credit unions, pension funds, insurance companies, and the like—that act as middlemen, transferring funds from original savers (or ultimate lenders) on one side of the counter to ultimate borrowers on the other. They borrow from Peter in order to lend to Paul. (Actually, they have been borrowing from Peter and lending to Paul so often that Paul is by now way over his head in debt; his credit rating ain't worth peanuts anymore.) What all financial intermediaries have in common is that they acquire funds by issuing their own liabilities to the public (savings deposits, savings and loan shares), and then they turn around and use this money to buy financial assets (stocks, bonds, mortgages) for themselves.

Because these institutions exist, savers who do not want to hoard their cash under a mattress, but who feel hesitant abut purchasing corporate bonds or stocks or mortgages because they feel that these assets are perhaps too risky or too illiquid, are given a third alternative. They can "purchase" savings deposits or savings and loan shares. In that way, they can hold a relatively safe and quite liquid financial asset, yet still earn *some* interest income. Nevertheless, corporations and potential home-owners can still sell their bonds, stocks, and mortgages—to the financial intermediaries rather than to the original savers themselves. Financial intermediaries, in brief, "intermediate" between original savers, on the one hand, and final borrowers, on the other.

Financial intermediation is precisely the above process: savers depositing funds with financial institutions rather than directly buying bonds or mortgages, and the financial institutions, in turn, doing the lending to the ultimate borrowers. Disintermediation is the reverse: savers taking funds out of deposit accounts, or reducing the amounts they normally put in, and investing directly, in their own name, in market securities such as stocks and bonds.

Financial Intermediation Lowers Interest Rates

As a general proposition, interest rates on securities (bonds, stocks, mortgages, and so forth) exist in order to induce the public to bear the risks inherent in owning them—risks such as potential capital losses due to interest-rate fluctuations, possible default, illiquidity, and so on. In other words, the borrower must pay the lender for parting with the most liquid of all assets, money, and holding in its place a relatively illiquid security.

Financial institutions are in a better position than individuals to bear and spread the risks of security ownership. Because of their large size, intermediaries can diversify their portfolios and minimize the risk involved in holding any one security. They are experts in evaluating borrower credit characteristics. They employ skilled portfolio managers and can take advantage of administrative economies in large-scale buying and selling.

For these reasons, they can afford to receive lower yields on their assets and will accept them if they have to. Competition among financial intermediaries forces interest rates to the lowest level that is compatible with their evaluation of the risks of security ownership. These yields are lower than if the same securities were held by individual investors, unable to minimize their risks so efficiently.

Looked at in another way, financial institutions also help to reduce the demand for money, thereby contributing to lower interest rates. People hold money both for day-to-day transactions and also for safety, because of the riskiness of stock or bond holding (relative to cash). But such intermediary liabilities as savings deposits and savings and loan shares are also safe, as safe as money, and virtually as liquid. Indeed, they are so safe and liquid that they are often called near-monies or money substitutes.

With such safe and liquid assets available—ones that earn interest to boot—people will have less desire to hold money itself. They can be almost as liquid (and also earn some interest) if they substitute savings deposits in place of some of their cash holdings. The money that people release and deposit in financial intermediaries will be used, in turn, by the intermediaries to buy bonds, mortgages, and so on. Thus additional money enters the bond market and bond prices are bid up (interest rates drop). The net effect of financial intermediation is to lower interest rates.

There are many ways of looking at this process. We have just seen that the demand for bonds goes up. With a given supply of bonds, the increased demand drives bond prices up. Alternatively, we have also seen that the demand for money falls. Since the supply of money remains unchanged (it is determined by the Federal Reserve), this means that the supply of money is now greater than the demand, which tends to lower interest rates. Still another indication of intermediation is revealed by the behavior of velocity. Spending on goods and services can be increased when intermediary liabilities rise, as formerly idle cash is made available to finance ultimate borrowers. And when spending (GNP) goes up, while the money supply does not, an increase in velocity results.

The growth in financial intermediaries has been spectacular in the last twenty-five years. Savings deposits in commercial banks have grown from $30 billion at the end of World War II to over $275 billion, and savings and loan shares have increased from less than $10 billion to over $180 billion. At the same time, we have experienced a general *increase* in the level of interest rates. This does not necessarily contradict what we have said above. If all other factors had remained the same, the growth in intermediation should have reduced interest rates. But, of course, all other factors have not remained the same.

Both the money supply and intermediary liabilities have been growing, providing us with increased liquidity. However, this has been more than absorbed both by the sus-

tained growth in the demand for funds by ultimate borrowers, floating more and more new bonds, and by the rise
in GNP and the price level, both of which have increased
the demand for cash for transactions purposes. The net
effect has been that the increase in the demand for liquidity has outpaced the increase in the supply of liquidity so
that interest rates have risen. In light of the volume of
borrowing and the rise in prices and GNP since World
War II, what is surprising, and must be attributed in large
part to the growth of intermediation, is that the rise in interest rates has not been considerably greater.

It is worth noting that since financial intermediation
tends to lower interest rates, or at least moderate any increase, it has been highly beneficial to our rate of economic
growth. A high rate of economic growth requires a heavy
volume of real investment. The lower the rate of interest
that ultimate borrowers must pay, the greater their expenditure on real investment is likely to be.

The beneficial effect of intermediation on economic
growth can also be seen from the viewpoint of risk-bearing.
Intermediaries are better able than individuals to bear the
risks of lending out venture capital. As was previously
stressed, ability to diversify, economies of scale, and expertise in lending account for this comparative advantage of
institutions over individuals. As financial intermediaries
own a larger and larger portion of the marketable securities
outstanding, the subjective risk borne by the economy is
lowered, interest rates are reduced, and more real investment takes place. Funds are channeled from ultimate
lenders, through intermediaries, to ultimate borrowers more
efficiently than if the intermediaries did not exist.

Intermediation and Monetary Policy

One of the most widely debated contributions to monetary theory and policy in recent years has come to be known as the Gurley-Shaw Thesis, after its originators and chief expositors, John Gurley and Edward Shaw, both of Stanford University.

Gurley and Shaw emphasize that the deposit liabilities of savings and loan associations, savings banks, and other financial intermediaries are, after all, not much different from the demand-deposit liabilities of commercial banks, even though we call only the latter money. It is true that we can spend demand deposits, and that we cannot spend a savings and loan share, at least not without cashing it in first. But cashing it in is a simple matter, easily accomplished; thus savings and loan shares and savings deposits, whether at commercial banks or at savings banks, are for all practical purposes almost as liquid as demand deposits.

Gurley and Shaw conclude that since these near-monies are outside the jurisdiction of the Federal Reserve, they make the successful execution of monetary policy difficult. Controlling liquidity only through the money supply will not work very well, since liquidity can also be provided by near-monies. Similarly, controlling the lending of commercial banks, which the Federal Reserve can do, will not accomplish much if the lending of all other financial intermediaries, over which the Federal Reserve has no direct control, is left unhampered.

According to Gurley and Shaw, the problem is especially acute in the case of anti-inflationary monetary policy. Assume the Federal Reserve reduces the money supply in order to inhibit spending on real and financial assets. Interest rates on market securities rise. Now the intermediaries go into action. Aware of the higher yields and the profits they imply, savings and loan associations raise the rate they offer on deposits in an effort to attract more funds, funds they can then invest in the higher-yielding securities. The increase in deposit rates induces some individuals to put more funds in savings banks, savings and loan associations, and the like. Financial intermediation is in full swing.

The individuals shifting money to the intermediaries may use funds they formerly had directly invested in securities, thus rebuilding their liquidity; and they may use what were idle money balances, now coaxed out of hiding by the attractive rates posted and widely advertised by the intermediaries. As long as the latter occurs to some extent, there will be a net expansion in the demand for market securities (by the intermediaries), a consequent moderation in the rise in interest rates, and—most important of all—the channeling of previously idle money balances into the eager hands of ultimate borrower-spenders.

With spending unchecked and the money supply curtailed, velocity will rise and everyone will say the Federal Reserve can't stop inflation because it can't control velocity. But Gurley and Shaw would say the Federal Reserve can't stop inflation because it can't control nonbank financial intermediation and the creation of near-monies.

The Gurley-Shaw hypothesis, which was first developed in the mid-1950s here and at about the same time in England by the Radcliffe Committee, appeared to be vindicated by the experience of the 1950s and early 1960s. At that time, tight money invariably was accompanied by the mobilization of idle balances, an expansion in intermediation by financial institutions other than commercial banks, and consequent financing of the boom by these intermediaries. Debate raged as to whether the Federal Reserve should have the power to set reserve requirements for savings banks and savings and loan associations, and congressional hearings were held to explore ways to solve the problem.

But perhaps the problem solved itself, or was solved accidentally. Because the tight money periods of 1966 and 1969 told a different story.

Disintermediation

During the tight money episodes of 1966 and 1969, market interest rates rose to what were then record levels, but the expected financial intermediation did not take place. Deposit rates did not go up as rapidly as open market rates on securities—and savers, instead of shifting funds *to* financial intermediaries, shifted them *out*. Individuals removed funds from savings accounts and put the money directly into corporate, municipal, and government securities. Financial *dis*intermediation!

This put the intermediaries under severe pressure. With substantial withdrawals and minimal inflows of new funds, their profit position was threatened, their solvency was endangered, and their ability to lend evaporated. They reacted as financial institutions will—by pulling in their horns, trying to retrench, and running to Congress for help. In other words, they aggravated tight money conditions instead of, as before, ameliorating them.

What happened?

Market rates went so high so fast that the intermediaries, for both internal and external reasons, could not raise the rates they pay depositors high enough or fast enough to stay competitive. Disappointed, depositors drowned their sorrow by going out and buying high-yielding securities on their own.

Two reasons prevented the intermediaries from sufficiently adjusting their deposit rates to stay competitive with open market rates. *Internally*, they felt they could not afford to. The assets of most intermediaries are primarily long term in nature; most were bought some time ago, at considerably lower yields. The average rate of return is thus heavily weighted by the past. The purchase of new, higher-yielding securities will only slightly increase the overall yield on the total portfolio. On the other hand, if they increase their deposit rates to attract new money, they have no choice but to pay the new higher rates to *all* depositors.

In 1966 and again in 1969, market rates moved up so far and so rapidly that most financial institutions felt, after a brief attempt to stay in the race, that it was too costly to continue. They had, to put it bluntly, been priced out of the market.

But there was another reason why they did not stay in the race, an *external* one. Some intermediaries—perhaps the better managed ones—were all for posting higher deposit rates and going after new business. But they couldn't. The legal rate ceilings, imposed by the Federal Reserve, the Federal Home Loan Bank Board, and other supervisory agencies, prevented them from raising deposit rates further once the maximum limits had been reached.

Indeed, in mid-1966 the deposit-rate ceilings were actually rolled back to lower levels, forcing many institutions that had posted higher interest rates to reduce them. With market rates still rising, it is no wonder depositors withdrew their money and went directly into the securities markets.

Deposit Rate Ceilings

The Federal Reserve sets the legal maximum interest rates —through what is known as Regulation Q—that commercial banks are allowed to pay on their time and savings deposit liabilities. The maximum interest rates that the savings banks and savings and loan associations may offer depositors are also regulated.

If these ceilings are set above going deposit rates, they are inoperative and irrelevant. But once deposit rates push up against the ceilings, they tend effectively to inhibit intermediation by preventing financial institutions from competing against open market securities for funds. To the extent that disintermediation results, open market rates will rise even higher than otherwise.

For this reason, when we are in a period of tight money and the regulatory authorities fail to raise Regulation Q and the comparable regulations over the other intermediaries (or actually lower the ceilings, as they did in 1966) they are making monetary policy even more restrictive. When Regulation Q and its counterparts are raised, as was always done prior to 1966, this is viewed as an easing sign.

This may seem a bit peculiar—considering the lowering of an interest rate to be a sign of tightness, the raising of a rate a sign of ease. Once the intermediation process is recognized, however, it is clear that a lowering of Q induces financial disintermediation, and thereby higher market interest rates; while an increase in Q promotes financial intermediation, and thereby lower market interest rates, especially long-term rates.

An increase in Q tends to make bank time deposits more attractive than competing, highly liquid, short-term financial instruments, such as Treasury bills. This may raise short-term interest rates on Treasury bills, as people and corporations shift from bills to deposits. But as the intermediaries, in turn, buy long-term financial assets with the funds, long rates tend to fall. Since investment spending by business firms is related primarily to long-term rates rather than short rates, the entire process is expansionary.

Regulation Q emerged rather late as a tool of monetary policy. When the Federal Reserve Act was passed in 1913, it contained no provision of any sort fixing maximum permissible interest rates that banks could pay on their time and savings deposits. At that time, this was not considered an appropriate area of regulation. Twenty years later, in 1933, Congress instructed the Federal Reserve to set such rate ceilings on commercial banks. However, the ceilings were always raised to higher levels whenever they became troublesome—until 1966. At that time, similar rate ceilings were imposed on competing deposit-type financial institutions and, instead of being raised, they were *lowered*.

The 1933 provision was enacted on the grounds that excessive interest-rate competition for deposits during the 1920s had undermined the soundness of the banking system. It was believed that competition among banks for funds had driven deposit rates up too high. To cover their costs, banks acquired high-yielding but excessively risky low-quality assets. This deterioration in the quality of bank portfolios, it was said, contributed to the collapse of the banking system in the early 1930s. Abolition of interest rate competition for deposits, by setting rate ceilings, was seen as rooting out the basic element weakening the banking system. Similar arguments were responsible for the imposition of comparable ceilings over other intermediaries starting in 1966.

This analysis is open to serious question. In retrospect, it is not at all clear that the historical experience on which Regulation Q was based was correctly interpreted at the time the legislation was enacted. Interest rates on bank time and savings deposits actually declined during the 1920's, and thorough investigation since has failed to substantiate any appreciable deterioration in the quality of bank assets during that period.

With respect to the early 1930s, what was once interpreted as a banking collapse due to mismanagement by commercial bankers now appears to be much more a case of banking collapse due to inadequate *central* banking. There is rather widespread agreement today that, had the Federal Reserve stepped in promptly and vigorously, the greater part of the banking debacle of the early 1930s could have been avoided.

Enthusiasm for Regulation Q probably reached its peak during the 1966 credit squeeze. One member of the Board of Governors of the Federal Reserve System went so far as to say that "Regulation Q was the cutting edge of monetary policy."

In its crudest form, the reason for wanting to add deposit rate ceilings to the weapons in the arsenal of monetary policy appears to be as follows. Monetary policy, as traditionally employed, frequently results in sharply higher interest rates. Such higher rates produce unpalatable side effects, such as a larger interest burden on the national debt, political repercussions, and possible distortions in the distribution of income, to mention only a few. It would be so much nicer if monetary policy could achieve its purposes without such side effects. Regulation Q to the rescue. Monetary policy without higher interest rates. Monetary policy without tears.

A somewhat more charitable interpretation would run along the following lines. The main objective of the central bank is to control the extension of bank credit. Regulation Q reinforces the bite of monetary policy by encouraging depositors to shift their funds *out* of commercial banks when market rates rise above the ceilings. This curtails the ability of banks to extend further credit and thereby reinforces the traditional instruments of monetary policy. (Notice that while the line of thinking in the previous paragraph involves keeping interest rates *low,* the argument in this paragraph is precisely the opposite—it involves *high* market interest rates as the inducement for financial disintermediation.)

By the time the 1969 credit crunch arrived, however, the banking system had devised numerous ways to soften the impact of Regulation Q; prevented by the rate ceilings from attracting deposits, bankers invented alternative sources of funds. They established holding companies that in turn issued commercial paper, borrowed funds from their European branches (see Chapter 20), and tapped a wide variety of other nondeposit sources to acquire lendable funds.

The lesson has become clear. Once the financial community recovered from the shock, it learned how to adjust to rate ceilings by locating and cultivating alternative (nonregulated) sources of funds. The Federal Reserve then had to try to plug these leaks by new regulations. What the Federal Reserve Bank of New York described as a "cat and mouse game" became the primary preoccupation of both commercial and central bankers. The effect of rate ceilings has become primarily the diversion of funds around the regulated areas and into those that are not (yet) regulated; the ceilings do not affect the aggregate flow of funds as much as they alter the course they take.

Regulation Q today appears to have its main impact not as an effective instrument of Federal Reserve policy, but as a competition-inhibiting element within the financial system, as we discuss in the following chapter.

16

THE STRUCTURE OF THE COMMERCIAL BANKING INDUSTRY

Commercial banks are the most important group of financial intermediaries in the United States. At the end of 1972, they had total assets amounting to $700 billion, as compared with $240 billion for life insurance companies, $240 billion for savings and loan associations, and $100 billion for savings banks. An industry this sizable, particularly one so intimately involved with the monetary and payments system, clearly occupies a key role in the functioning of the economy.

Is the banking industry so structured as to best provide the financial services needed by a changing and growing economy? For example, does a borrower who is refused a loan at one bank generally have other viable options open to him, other banks to which he can turn? Similarly, are the opportunities open to a depositor sufficiently varied to give him an array of choices with respect to deposit terms and yields, so that he can shop around for those that best fit his particular circumstances? In other words, is there enough competition in banking to make it a dynamic and innovative industry, responsive to private needs and public goals?

Deposit Rate Ceilings Again

Probably the most competition-inhibiting element in banking at the present time is our old friend Regulation Q, the legal prohibition against banks paying depositors more than a specified maximum interest rate on time and savings deposits. As noted in the previous chapter, interest rate ceilings were enacted in 1933 on the questionable premise that excessive rate competition for deposits had undermined the soundness of the banking system.

Whatever the logic of such ceilings in 1933, after a period of thousands of bank failures, there are fewer grounds for continuing them today, in the considerably different environment of the 1970s. Bank failures are now rare—over the past quarter century they have averaged less than six a year—and those that have occurred have generally been attributable not to competitive pressures but to embezzlement or similar fraudulent practices. The reason so few banks have failed lies not in the existence of Regulation Q but in the presence of the Federal Deposit Insurance Corporation. By insuring deposits under the auspices of the federal government, the FDIC has successfully eliminated the "run on the bank" by frightened depositors that invariably culminated in a bank failure in the 1920s and early 1930s.

What Regulation Q *does* do, however, is effectively prevent aggressive, well-managed banks from offering depositors more attractive interest rates than the bank next door. Aggressive banks that would like to compete for funds, by bidding more for deposits, are legally prohibited from doing so. Which also means, of course, that depositors are simultaneously deprived of the enlarged options that more vigorous price competition among banks would offer them. It is quite true that banks have been known to give away toasters, radios, and a two-year subscription to *Playboy* in order to attract savings deposits. But how do banks reach those who don't eat bread, can't stand the radio, and have foresworn serious reading?

In addition, Regulation Q discriminates against the small depositor. Higher interest rates are permitted on larger deposits (over $100,000) than on smaller ones. During the early 1970s, for example, the most a small depositor could legally get at a commercial bank was 5¾ percent, although it was permissible for the same bank to pay a large depositor up to 7½ percent. When frustrated small depositors tried to shift over to Treasury bills in 1970, joining the crowd in financial disintermediation, the U.S. Treasury showed whose side *it* was on by promptly raising the minimum Treasury bill denomination from $1,000 to $10,000.

Closely related to Regulation Q on time and savings deposits is the legal prohibition that exists against banks paying any interest at all on demand deposits—in effect, a demand-deposit interest-rate ceiling set at zero. The reasoning behind this legislation, which was also enacted in 1933, is similar to that behind Q—as are the objections to it.

The right to deal in checking accounts evidently has some value. If it did not, commercial banks would not be so eager to get them and savings banks and savings and loan associations would not be lobbying for the right to do the same. Under such circumstances, it is reasonable to expect that if competition were unfettered some bankers would bid, via interest payments, to attract demand deposits. As matters now stand, this source of funds is acquired at no cost, for free, which is nice for bankers but not so nice for depositors. Actually, banks do compete for demand deposits by providing their customers with checks that have their names on them and sometimes even with pretty pictures. This certainly costs the banks money. But wouldn't we all be better off if the banks offered us cash instead—in the form of interest payments? Some people might prefer money over art, strange as that might seem.

One function of financial institutions is to offer as broad as possible a spectrum of liabilities, thereby enlarging the options available to potential depositors. At present, because of the zero interest rate ceiling on demand deposits, there is a gap in the alternatives—the option of an interest-bearing demand deposit. If any depositor wants that option and any bank wants to provide it, both would presumably be better off were they permitted to come to terms.

Branching and New Entry

While deposit interest-rate ceilings are probably the most important factor restraining competition in banking today, they are run a close second by the network of laws and regulations regarding branch banking and new entry into the industry.

There are over 13,500 independent banks in the United States, which would appear to indicate, on the face of it, a high degree of robust competition. However, closer scrutiny reveals that 7,000 of them are in one-bank towns and another 2,000 in two-bank communities. Almost all of these 9,000 banks are very small institutions, each with less than $25 million in deposits. Indeed, fully 11,000 of the 13,500 banks in the country—80 percent of them—are that small.

If this large number of very small banks were the product of natural evolution, it would indicate that the optimum (low cost) size bank is probably in that neighborhood, and it would attest to the competitive viability of such institutions. However, the fact of the matter is that banks so small as $25 million in deposits or less are far from the most profitable size category. It is banks in the $100–500-million-size classification that typically lead all the rest in terms of net income after taxes as a percent of capital, thus indicating that the optimum size bank is most likely somewhere in that range.

The reason there are so many very small banks in this country does not have very much to do with their profitability, with their successful adaptation to changing economic needs, or with their innovative capabilities. It is simply because most of them are *sheltered* from competition by state antibranching statutes, to which the federal banking authorities defer. Most small banks would be too inefficient to remain in business were a large bank to open up a branch next door. The fact that in many states the large bank is legally prohibited from doing so is all that permits most small banks to survive—and to saddle their communities with high-cost banking.

Fifteen states, mostly in the Midwest, permit only unit banking—that is, no branch banking is allowed at all. Sixteen states, mostly in the East, allow only some limited form of branching. Nineteen states, largely in the West, permit unlimited statewide branching. Federal regulations require that a federally chartered bank abide by the branching laws of the state in which it is operating, and interstate branching is prohibited everywhere. Well over half the banks in the country are located in the fifteen unit-banking states, where the average bank size is only about one-fifth that in unlimited branching states.

Thus it is state antibranching statutes, not economic circumstances, that are the principal determinant of the number of banks in the United States. The fact that there are over 13,500 commercial banks bears witness to the absence, not the presence, of vigorous competition. If there were fewer banks, and more of them were closer to optimum size, the general public would be better served.

Most state legislatures that have maintained strict antibranching statutes have done so in the face of overwhelming evidence that branching would be more efficient and more viable in providing the financial services needed by a dynamic economy. This has become more important recently than it has ever been, with the introduction of large-scale computerized technology into banking; even present, not to mention future, technology cannot be utilized advantageously by small unit banks, where the costs are too great because volume is too small. However, the political influence of the banking industry on the state level has repeatedly outflanked the interests of the (unorganized) general public, a process that has been facilitated by the tactic of playing on the deep-seated American fear of bigness, especially in banking (the Bigness Complex, inherited by American sons from their Mothers).

Apparently there is only one realistic way to initiate meaningful change in this area, and that is by removing federal deference to state branching statutes—permitting federally chartered banks, in other words, to branch over a specified area regardless of state law. Under such competitive pressures, the states can be expected to accelerate the granting of similar rights to institutions chartered by themselves.

Closely related to the branching issue is that of new entry into the banking industry. By law, both federal and state banking authorities typically evaluate a number of conditions before chartering a new bank. These include the adequacy of its capital structure, the general character of its management, its future earnings prospects, the convenience and needs of the community it proposes to serve. (Further, the well-known liquidity index is given due consideration: namely, the number of state legislators on the bank's board of directors multiplied by the number of little league baseball teams it proposes to sponsor.)

Few would dispute the necessity of maintaining standards of capital adequacy, or the need for determining that the management of a proposed new bank, and their backers, are honest people, without underworld connections. (Not to mention the desirability of a rating higher than 3π on the liquidity index.) But the other two elements in the screening process, the future earnings prospects of the proposed new bank and the convenience and needs of the community in which it would be located, in effect shield existing banking institutions from the rigors (and vitality) of competition more than they serve the interests of the public at large.

The purpose of both an earnings prospects criterion and a convenience and needs criterion is said to be the prevention of bank failures. But measures that insulate all banks from the slightest chance of failure are also measures that inhibit risk-taking, discourage financial innovation, circumscribe management decision-making, and stifle the benefits to the general public that can flow from competitive rivalry. These are high costs to pay, particularly when federal deposit insurance protection has eliminated the widespread distress that bank failures formerly caused.

One recent proposal would quickly and dramatically increase the number of new entrants into the commercial banking industry. Early in 1972, President Nixon's Commission on Financial Structure and Regulation recommended that all savings and loan associations and savings banks that want to do so, and are qualified, be permitted, in effect, to become commercial banks. Were Congress to pass the enabling legislation, we could have 6,000 more commercial banks at the stroke of a pen. But if 13,500 commercial banks is already too many, would 19,500 be an improvement?

Do the Giant Banks Pose a Monopoly Threat?

So far we have emphasized that there are too many small banks in the United States, with 11,000 of the 13,500 banks in the country—80 percent of them—too small for efficient operation. However, these 80 percent of the banks, all under $25 million in deposit size, hold only 20 percent of the deposits in the banking system.

What about at the other end of the scale: the 14 Giant Banks, each of which has over $5 *billion* in deposits? This handful of banks, one-tenth of 1 percent of all the banks in the country, holds more than 25 percent of all the banking system's deposits—more deposits than are in *all* the 11,000 small banks put together. Do these 14 Giants pose a clear and present monopoly danger?

Opinions differ on this, of course, but at this stage in history the Giant Banks appear to be more benign than malignant. Not because they are particularly generous, home-loving, or patriotic—at least no more so than you and I—but simply because, large as they are, they still face sufficient competition to keep them in line. Close on their heels are another 55 banks, with deposits between $1 and $5 billion, and close behind *them* come another 50 or so with deposits between $500 million and a billion. Indeed, *all* of these banks may be too large to operate at maximum efficiency, as evidenced by the fact that the most profitable banks, as we mentioned before, are typically in the next lower size category, $100–500 million of deposits.

The monopoly threat is further ameliorated in this country by legislation that forbids banking and industrial operations by the same firm. In many other countries— Japan is the outstanding example—giant banks are affiliated with giant manufacturing firms under common ownership, representing a vast concentration of economic power. If Chase Manhattan Bank, Xerox and IBM could merge into one huge combine, as is permissible in Japan, then we would really have something to worry about.

None of the above should be taken to advocate complacency. Advances in technology are likely to increase the optimum size of bank in the future, as well as generate powerful economic incentives for mergers between banks and other kinds of business—especially with those involved in data transmission and communications. Nevertheless, so long as existing antitrust statutes are enforced, fears of the dangers of banking monopoly appear, at least at the present time, to be unrealistic.

PART VI

Money and National Priorities

17

FINANCIAL RESOURCES, REAL

RESOURCES, AND NATIONAL

PRIORITIES

Probably the most overworked sentence in the political lexicon of the past few years is "We must reorder our national priorities." Wrung dry by politicians of all persuasions, it has become one of the most ubiquitous clichés of our times. Add the thought-substitute "ya know" and you have summed up a considerable portion of the vocabulary of no small segment of our population.

Although "ya know" still leaves us unenlightened, and we leave it to the psychiatrists to analyze what is being covered up, we feel it is important for a book about money to uncover the dollar implications of "reordering our national priorities." When most people use the phrase, what they seem to be saying is that the United States has serious internal problems that demand attention. Problems such as poverty, urban blight, crime, pollution, and the like. Typically, that is the end of the story, except for apocalyptic visions of what is likely to happen if *something* isn't done. No attempt is made to quantify what has to be done, however. What dollar amounts are involved? Who

will foot the bill? Priorities are by nature relative: if some
are raised higher, then mustn't others be dropped lower?

Quantifying Reordered Priorities

What are our most urgent specific needs and what are their
financial dimensions? Aside from the direct reduction of
poverty, which we shall return to later, there appears to be
general agreement that additional resources should be
devoted to (a) improving mass transit in urban and
suburban areas; (b) curbing environmental pollution; (c)
providing better housing for low-income families; (d)
improving police protection, law enforcement, and the
judicial and penal systems generally; (e) upgrading the
quality of education, particularly that available to minority-
group children; and (f) bettering the quantity and quality
of medical research and health care, especially its availability to the aged and to low- and middle-income groups.

It has become abundantly clear that none of these problem areas can be resolved simply by spending more money,
any more than purely military means ever succeeded in
resolving the Vietnam quagmire. "Spend more money" is a
first cousin to "Send more troops." It is equally true, however, that improvements cannot realistically be expected
unless more money is indeed spent. At present, estimates
of the dollar amounts needed to make significant headway in these areas are little more than guesswork (and
even less thought has been devoted to least-cost methods of
realizing objectives). Nevertheless, the crude calculations
that have been made can give a rough idea of the financial
magnitudes involved. Take out your pencil, because here
come some numbers—lots of them.

Conservative estimates require the following *additional* spending: $5 billion a year at (1971 prices) to improve mass transit; $10 billion a year more to make meaningful progress toward pollution control; $10 billion a year more for low- and middle-income housing; $15 billion additonal annually for law enforcement and judicial-penal reform; $20 billion annually toward nationwide school reform; and another $20 billion a year for appropriate health care and medical research. This package adds up to a total of $80 billion *a year* more for these purposes than we, as a nation, are currently spending.

How does this stack up against existing priorities? In 1971, for example, 63 percent of our national output was in the form of consumer goods and services, 11 percent was capital goods (business investment spending), and 7 percent went for federal defense. These are the Favored Priorities: they command 81 percent of our total output of goods and services. The remaining 19 percent of GNP are the Ugly Duckling Priorities—state and local government spending (13 percent), housing (4 percent), and federal nondefense purchases of goods and services (2 percent).

Almost all of the $80 billion a year, or 7½ percent of 1971's GNP, needed to *reorder* priorities falls into the Ugly Duckling class—in the main, they are either state and local government functions, housing, or federal government nondefense functions (either by tradition or because of default on the part of private enterprise). A meaningful reordering of national priorities implies taking 7½ percent of our national output away from the Favored Priorities and moving it over to the Ugly Ducklings. A real reordering of priorities, as opposed to liberal lip-service, is clearly no trivial matter.

Peace and Growth Dividends

Many advocates of reordering priorities think that it can be done with little pain, that a post-Vietnam "peace dividend" and a normal "growth dividend" will magically supply all the needed $80 billion. They are not altogether wrong. Peace and growth can help, but they alone will not be enough. As economists have observed time and again, there is no such thing as a free lunch—you always wind up paying for it, in one way or another.

A post-Vietnam peace dividend, for example, is defined as the resources that would be released by a pull-back in federal defense spending to 1965 levels, prior to the massive build-up in Southeast Asia. In 1965, defense expenditures were $50 billion; in 1971, they were $72 billion. Simple subtraction yields an apparent $22-billion annual windfall after the war. But such calculations are oversimplified, because they fail to take into account the inflation that has taken place since 1965. If the government today were to try to buy the same *real* defense package it paid $50 billion for in 1965, prior to the Vietnam build-up, the price tag would now run to approximately $67 billion— leaving a "windfall" of only $5 billion a year for alternative uses. This is small potatoes when set against the $80 billion that is needed.

What about the possible contribution of economic growth, the ability of our economy to expand its productive capacities over a period of time? The most optimistic forecasts for the coming decade anticipate a real growth rate averaging no more than 5 percent a year. If realized, this would yield additional real output averaging about $65 billion a year every year during the 1970s. But the process of growth does no more than make about $65 billion of additional resources available every year, which are then up for grabs. If state and local spending, housing, and federal nondefense spending—the Ugly Ducklings—continue to receive the same shares of the pie as they do now, which total 19 percent, then growth alone will provide only 19 percent of the $65 billion annual expansion in output for those purposes, or an incremental $12 billion a year every year.

At best, then, a peace dividend could contribute only $5 billion a year toward the $80 billion needed, a growth dividend $12 billion additional each year. Together, they add up to only $17 billion the first year after the war is over, $29 billion the next year, $41 billion the year after that, and so on. It would take more than six years to reach the requisite $80 billion, and by that time neglect would have swollen the required amount. While we may not preach "instant gratification," neither do we endorse "benign neglect."

Deliberate Resource Reallocation

If we are truly to reorder priorities, we thus have no choice but deliberately to use governmental policies to *reallocate* some resources. If the Ugly Duckling Priorities are to get more, some of the Favored Priorities will have to get less. The only questions are what to cut and by how much.

A favorite starting point for radical surgery is usually business plant and equipment spending (11 percent of GNP in 1971). Let the giant corporations pull in their belts; aren't they already too big? Hit the Fat Cats where it hurts, below the pocketbook. But this approach is likely to be self-defeating. (Sorry about that.) Unless business firms continue to build and improve their plant and equipment, productivity will falter and the 5 percent growth rate in GNP will be one more unfulfilled prophecy. The result would be a smaller-than-$12-billion annual growth dividend, thereby compounding our difficulties.

This leaves federal defense (7 percent of GNP) and consumer spending (63 percent) as the only candidates left for contraction. (So what else is new?) To realize a reordering of priorities, it all comes down to not *whether* to cut back on defense and/or consumer spending but to *how* and in what proportions. If national defense absorbs the entire decline, then consumer spending can remain unaffected. But national security requirements may prevent meaningful reductions in the defense budget, and then consumer spending will have to take the brunt of the squeeze. In the 1970s, given reordered priorities and reasonably full employment, every additional dollar spent on guns will mean a dollar less for butter. (The old guns-and-butter problem that has helped Paul Samuelson sell two and a half million copies of his textbook.)

All of this suggests that consumer spending will indeed have to be curbed, in order to feed the Ugly Ducklings. This could be undertaken through a variety of governmental measures, including most prominently higher tax rates (don't laugh—pretty soon you'll be paying your share) and selective credit controls. We look at both of these methods in the remainder of this chapter.

Reordered Priorities Mean Higher Taxes

The standard way to influence total consumer outlays is by varying tax rates—lowering them to encourage and raising them to discourage consumer spending. Higher tax rates thus emerge as the painful counterpart of reordered priorities. It is precisely here that the American public's desire for a true reordering of priorities will meet its severest test, because any significant restraint on consumer spending must necessarily imply higher taxes on middle-income families. As a practical matter, reduced consumption simply cannot be accomplished primarily by increasing taxes on business or the wealthy.

Higher business taxes are likely to inhibit investment rather than consumer spending. But business investment in new plant and equipment, as emphasized above, is needed for an adequate growth rate. Despite recent questioning of some of the byproducts of economic growth, the fact remains that it is still the most important single generator of usable resources. Tokyo psychiatrists have recommended that after a hard day at the office the trip home on the crowded train must be a sedative: they prescribe getting as close as possible to a member of the opposite sex. (Don't ask why corporations would expand to produce more when consumers are buying less. The answer is that business firms don't care who their customers are; increased spending by state and local governments, and so on, would replace what would have been spent by consumers.)

"Soaking the rich" is no answer either. Raising taxes on the rich, say on those with annual incomes over $50,000, might be justifiable on the grounds of equity, but it is not likely to go far toward the objective of reducing consumer spending. The rich do not account for that much consumer spending in the first place, and in any event, of all taxpayers, they would be the most likely to react to higher taxes by cutting back their saving rather than their spending. Nor, of course, can any help be expected from reducing the consumption of those already at or close to the subsistence level.

The conclusion is inescapable: a large share of the cost of reordered priorities (less consumption) will have to be borne (in taxes) by middle-income families; it is they who comprise the bulk of the population and who do most of the consumer spending.

An alternative to explicitly higher tax rates is the *implicit* tax that is imposed through inflation. Increased spending on the Ugly Ducklings without reductions in either defense or consumer spending is likely to strain the economy's productive capacity and to drive prices higher. The result generally is to contract most the consumption of those least able to protect themselves, such as the elderly and the fringe workers in nonunionized employment.

Finally, there is the direct attack on poverty per se. This is somewhat different from the kind of things we have mentioned so far. Pollution control, upgrading the quality of education, and so forth involve the shifting of resources from one category of spending to another. The objective of income maintenance programs, on the other hand, is not to direct spending to particular uses but to direct income to particular persons: the main effect would be a redistribution within the total of consumer spending, from upper income groups toward lower.

It has been estimated by the Census Bureau that direct action to bring all Americans up to the subsistence level, via some plan of family allowances or negative income taxes, would cost approximately $11 billion a year. Again, this would have to be financed in substantial part by taxes on middle-income families, because that is where most of the income is.

Can Selective Credit Controls Help?

Taxes hurt. You have to dig into your pocket—aggravating your tennis elbow. They may also inhibit work incentives, as we saw in Chapter 13, reducing aggregate production and economic well-being. Politicians, long aware of the unpopularity of higher taxes, have sought a less painful way to reorder national priorities.

Selective credit policies are the politicians' favorite alternative to taxation in reallocating resources among different uses. Such policies include prohibitory regulations regarding certain uses of credit, such as the consumer credit and real estate credit controls of the Korean War; favored legal status to lenders who make certain types of loans, such as the favorable tax treatment received by savings and loan associations as a quid pro quo for their concentrating on mortgage lending and the line of credit at the Treasury granted to the Federal National Mortgage Association in exchange for operating a secondary market in mortgages; and interest rate subsidies to certain categories of borrowers for making particular kinds of expenditures, such as students who are borrowing from banks to finance their education and poor families who are taking out mortgages to finance the purchase of homes.

This list only scatches the surface of the myriad of selective credit policies currently on the books in the United States. At last count, there were over fifty general categories of federal credit programs in operation, and that count did not include either the usury laws or the regulations imposed on financial institutions to channel credit into particular uses, such as the portfolio restrictions on savings and loan associations and the various legal lending limits imposed on commercial banks.

New selective credit policies are, in fact, being proposed all the time. For example, Andrew Brimmer, a member of the Board of Governors of the Federal Reserve System, has suggested that banks be required to have different reserve ratios on various categories of loans—higher ratios to discourage unfavored types of loans and lower ratios to encourage favored types.

At this point it is appropriate to ask at least four questions: (1) How are selective credit policies supposed to work? (2) Do they in fact work successfully? (3) What's wrong with them? (4) Why are they so popular?

A Catechism on Selective Credit Policies

QUESTION. *How are selective credit policies supposed to work?*

ANSWER. Their objective is to encourage (or discourage) a particular type of real expenditure—say, housing (or consumer durable goods expenditures)—by increasing (or decreasing) the volume of credit directed to such activities and/or by making the terms of credit (interest rates, downpayments) easier (or more stringent). One obvious prerequisite for the effectiveness of selective credit policies is that there be a close relationship between a specific type of credit and a particular category of real expenditure. For example, as long as the purchase of a home is closely related to the availability of mortgage credit it is possible to encourage housing by inducing lenders to make mortgage loans rather than other types of loans. As lenders devote more funds to mortgages and less, say, to business loans, the interest rate on mortgages should fall in relation to the rate on business loans, and people will thus be encouraged to take out mortgages and buy new homes.

But that is not the only way to use mortgage money. What if someone already has enough cash to buy a home and is ready to spend it for that purpose regardless of mortgage terms? The availability of cheap mortgage money then induces him to take out a mortgage to finance his home—freeing his other funds for more serious endeavors, like a two-year tour of the world's major red-light districts. In this case a house is not a home, and it is the former that the selective credit policy winds up financing!

A selective credit policy will be most effective in redirecting real resources when there is a rigid dollar-for-dollar relationship between a specific type of credit and a particular category of expenditure. To the extent that there is some slippage—that is, as long as the expenditure can be financed in other ways or as long as the specific type of credit can be used differently—the effectiveness of the selective credit policy is impaired.

Many selective credit policies are imposed on only one sector of the financial markets. The portfolio restrictions imposed on savings and loan associations, for example, limit their assets essentially to government bonds and mortgages, and as another example Governor Brimmer has made a proposal that commercial banks have different reserve requirements on different types of loans. Such selective credit policies increase the flow of credit to the favored uses only so long as other (unrestricted) lenders in financial markets do not counteract their behavior. For instance, if Brimmer's proposal is implemented and the reserve requirement against mortgage loans is low while the reserve requirement against consumer installment loans is high, banks will find it profitable to divert more funds to mortgages and less to consumer installment credit. Initially, mortgage rates will decline and consumer credit rates will go up. This is precisely the desired objective of the selective credit policy. *But* the reaction of other institutional lenders, such as life insurance companies, will then be to make fewer mortgage loans and to expand credit to consumer installment loans, which will ultimately tend to offset the impact of the selective policy. As long as this offset is incomplete, however, selective credit policies on only a few sectors of the credit market can successfully divert some funds into favored uses.

QUESTION. *Do they in fact work successfully?*

ANSWER. Under most circumstances, selective credit policies do seem to work. Imposing regulations and controls does appear to succeed in diverting credit into desired channels. Furthermore, borrowers do tend, for the most part, to use certain types of credit for specific types of real expenditures. But as we saw near the end of Chapter 15, in our discussion of Regulation Q, participants in financial markets are very creative when it comes to circumventing regulations. The very success of selective credit controls is likely to sow the seeds of their ultimate failure. If consumers cannot get credit from banks to finance the purchase of automobiles because, say, the banks are preoccupied with sewage bonds of local municipalities, then the auto dealers will arrange the necessary financing. How? Most probably through the auto manufacturers, who can float bonds in the capital markets and use the proceeds for anything they want, including extending loans to potential customers.

QUESTION. *What's wrong with selective credit policies?*

ANSWER. For one thing, as indicated in the preceding paragraph, in time their effectiveness tends to wear out. Another drawback is that the real costs of such programs are obscured by the financial maze. The unavoidable fact of life is that there is no such thing as a free lunch—when we are already at full employment the cost of more resources in education or housing has to be fewer resources available for other things. This lesson is brought home loud and clear when taxes must be raised to deter the other types of expenditure, with the proceeds going to the favored groups.

But favoring some borrowers (and thereby in effect squeezing others out of the credit market), while less direct than taxation, has similar social costs—less of something else. If politicians are not aware of these costs (and the proliferation of credit programs makes it doubtful that they are), then the indiscriminate use of selective credit policies tries to favor everyone and everything and winds up producing nothing.

QUESTION. *Why are selective credit policies so popular?*

ANSWER. Partly because they don't *seem* to be as painful as taxation. Those who are unable to buy new cars because they can't get financing are likely to blame fate or the world in general, while those who can't buy them because they have so little left after taxes are likely to blame the politicians in power. Also, more positively, selective credit policies do have the attractive feature of making the private sector an active partner in the process of redirecting resources. The government only provides the incentive—an interest subsidy, insurance for the lender against default, or some other feature. The bulk of the funds are still channeled through nongovernmental institutions.

The scope of activities currently receiving favorable treatment in the credit markets extends from exports and foreign economic development to community redevelopment and higher education. Housing, however, stands head-and-shoulders above all other activities as the spending category receiving the most credit favors. In the next chapter we explore the housing situation in detail, with special reference to the impacts of monetary policy and selective credit programs on home-building.

18

DOES TIGHT MONEY

DISCRIMINATE AGAINST

HOUSING?

Countercyclical monetary policy has often been accused of having "discriminatory" effects on the housing market. It is argued that tight money has its greatest impact on residential construction. In boom periods, when money is tightened and interest rates rise, home-building gets strangled. Subsequently, in recessions, when money eases and interest rates fall, home-building zooms ahead at an unnaturally rapid pace.

As a result, employment in the construction industry is unstable; workers try to even out their incomes over time by restrictive entry requirements and work rules; and entrepreneurs are discouraged from mechanization and modernization. All of which, it is alleged, leads to lower productivity in the housing industry than elsewhere in the economy. We are in the last half of the twentieth century but still building homes as though we were in the first half of the nineteenth. Low-cost housing seems impossible to construct and rents across the board, on both new and existing dwellings, are higher than they need be.

Is home-building indeed that fickle? If so, why? Can anything be done about it? *Should* anything be done about it?

The Truth about Housing

On the basis of the evidence, the contention that home-building is a foul-weather friend is difficult to deny. When GNP is bursting at the seams, construction tends to slacken; during downturns in overall business activity, the housing industry tends to expand. Of all the components of GNP, the record indicates that residential construction has experienced the greatest cyclical variability during the pastwar years.

The accompanying chart traces residential construction as a percent of GNP from 1951 through 1971. The shaded areas represent periods of recession in general business conditions, from the peaking out of the boom at the start of the shaded area to the trough of the recession at the end.

Home-building typically starts up during, or in some cases shortly after, a recession. Each of the shaded recession areas shows home-building swinging up except for 1960–61, and in that case it started to rise within a few months after the recession trough had been reached. Peaks in home construction occurred in 1955, 1959, 1963, and again in 1971—in other words, shortly after the recession—easy money years of 1954, 1958, 1961, and 1970.

On the other hand, during those years of highest overall employment and bubbling prosperity, usually accompanied by tight money, which are typically the years just *before* the shaded areas, residential construction is generally taking a nosedive. These boom periods are the very years

New Housing Expenditures as a Percent of GNP, 1951-71

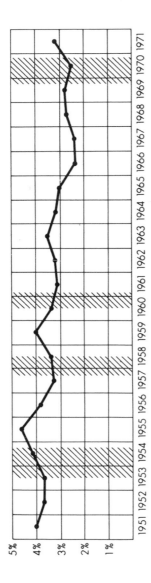

when other kinds of spending, for example, consumer durables and business plant and equipment, are generally at or near their peak. Bt housing does not follow suit. As resources turn to making automobiles, television sets, and machine tools, the construction of homes takes a back seat. Indeed, the impact of the credit crunch of 1966 on home-building was so great that housing starts dropped to a twenty-year low despite a record number of family formations; sales of existing homes fell off, and a great many contractors and realtors went out of business.

Why? What causes these fluctuations in the housing market, fluctuations that appear to be so closely related to the actions of the central bank?

The Instability of Supply

During periods of tight money and rising interest rates, the supply of funds to the mortgage market is drastically curtailed. This sharp reduction in funds available for home financing can be traced primarily to the inability of the major mortgage lenders, savings and loan associations and mutual savings banks, to compete for funds as interest rates rise. As we saw in Chapter 15, when interest rates rise during a period of tight money these institutions can compete for funds only so long as they can continue to move their deposit rates up in tandem with market rates. But two reasons prevent them from doing so for very long.

First, the assets of these institutions are primarily long term. Only a small portion of their portfolio turns over during any one year. Hence, when interest rates go up, they can receive a higher yield on only a small portion of their assets. Some of these financial institutions thus find it too costly to raise their deposit rates by as much as the increase in yields on government, municipal, and corporate bonds. Second, while many of the better-managed institutions might be willing to raise their deposit rates to maintain their inflow of funds, after a while they are prevented from doing so by the legal interest rate ceilings imposed on deposit rates.

As market rates continue to advance, but deposit rates at savings institutions do not, then savers—potential depositors—start to find it more attractive to invest their funds directly in the capital markets, rather than depositing them in savings and loans or savings banks. Financial disintermediation!

Since individual investors are not large mortgage lenders, funds that might well have gone into the mortgage market had they been deposited in a savings and loan association now move directly into stocks or bonds. The supply of funds available for mortgage lending dries up. This occurred most dramatically in 1966, when the savings and loan associations and savings banks lost funds not only to direct investment but also to the commercial banks, and again in 1969 when all deposit-type financial institutions (including commercial banks) were hard hit by financial disintermediation.

All this is only half the story. Another side of the coin, the nature of the *demand* for mortgage loans, also contributes to the instability of residential construction.

The Sensitivity of Demand

In Chapter 5 we noted that residential construction spending appears to be much more sensitive to changes in interest rates than any other category of expenditure. In the Federal Reserve–MIT–Penn econometric model of the economy, a one percentage point increase in long-term interest rates reduces housing expenditures by $3 billion after one year, while business plant and equipment spending is reduced barely half a billion dollars.

Why is the demand for housing so much more sensitive to changes in interest rates than other kinds of spending? There are probably two major reasons. First, interest is a much greater proportion of total outlay in home-buying than it is in shorter-lived investments, such as inventory investment or the purchase of manufacturing equipment. The longer the investment period—that is, the longer the money will be tied up in the investment—the larger interest costs loom as an element in total costs. As we noted in Chapter 7, if you buy a $20,000 home and obtain a mortgage for the full amount at 7 percent interest for thirty years, you will be paying $28,000 in *interest alone*. If the mortgage rate rises to 8 percent, this will add an additional $5,000.

Second, the demand for housing is probably more sensitive than other kinds of spending to interest rate changes because it is families that are undertaking the investment rather than business firms, and families can more easily postpone such expenditures for a year or two. Business firms also invest in long-lived projects—heavy machinery, physical plant, and so on—in which interest costs bulk as large as they do in housing. But corporations face competitive pressures from rival sellers and frequently have no choice in the matter; often they must either make improvements and additions quickly or else risk losing their share of the market.

Although it is difficult to pinpoint such things, the contraction in housing during 1952–53 and 1956–57 (see the chart) appears to have been due primarily to the interest sensitivity of demand. There was no sharp reduction in savings flows to intermediaries during those two tight-money periods, hence no major reduction in the availability of mortgage funds attributable to that source.

In 1966, however, the downturn in construction was significantly reinforced by a virtual stoppage in the supply of mortgage money. The diversion of savings flows away from mortgage-minded institutions and into direct market purchases of securities—financial disintermediation—is evident from even a casual inspection of the data. In 1965, savings and loan associations received $8.5 billion in deposits; in 1966, they received only $3.6 billion. Mutual savings banks experienced a similar decline. In fact, just about all the net additions to deposits at these institutions during 1966 represented interest payments credited to already existing accounts, rather than an inflow of new money.

The reaction of home buyers to changes in interest rates thus reinforces the reaction of potential suppliers of mortgage money. When rates fall or rise, home buyers revise their spending plans and lenders rethink their allocation of funds. Result: feast or famine in the building industry.

Fanny Mae and Her Friends

Since housing is high on our list of national priorities and since it is, in part, the government's use of countercyclical monetary policy (producing wide swings in interest rates) that causes instability in the housing industry, there has been considerable governmental effort to reduce the variability of home-building. Almost all this effort takes the form of selective credit policies designed to ameliorate the impact of tight money on housing.

The *Federal National Mortgage Association*, more widely known as Fanny Mae, is a government-sponsored institution that operates a secondary market in mortgages; more importantly, Fanny Mae buys mortgages when there is a shortage of private funds. Fanny is aided in the purchase of mortgages by her cousin (so she says), Ginny Mae (*Government National Mortgage Association*), which is part of the Department of Housing and Urban Development. Things get even more interesting when we introduce another government-sponsored agency, the Federal Home Loan Bank System, which makes loans to savings and loan associations—permitting them to borrow in large amounts to offset declines in deposits during periods of tight money. Now that, by itself, isn't so interesting, except that the Federal Home Loan Bank System was given a subsidiary by Congress in 1970—namely, the Federal Home Loan Mortgage Corporation, which also buys mortgages during periods of tight money. Still not especially interesting? But wait. Wall Street, which handles the securities that these agencies issue to finance their purchases of mortgages, has dubbed the 1970 addition to the mortgage-market fan club, Freddie Mac. Are the Wall Streeters just male chauvinist pigs, or do they know something about these three that can only be discussed behind closed doors and drawn curtains?

All these government and government-sponsored agencies are very active during periods of tight money. During 1969, both Fanny Mae and the Federal Home Loan Bank

System pumped large volumes of funds into the mortgage market. This is surely part of the reason that housing starts did not decline as sharply during the disintermediation of 1969 compared with the disintermediation of 1966, when both agencies were operating at a much lower scale.

There has been much concern in the money and capital markets, however, over the growth of federal credit programs. As we saw in the previous chapter, if one use of credit is favored, some other use will have to be cut back. As federally sponsored agencies bid for funds in the credit market by issuing their own securities (in order to buy mortgages), other borrowers without federal backing are squeezed out. It is those who are squeezed out (the squeezees) who bear the burden of tight money and higher interest rates.

Should this massive federal credit effort be made to stabilize the mortgage market? It is not such a bad thing, once you think about it, for the economy to have a foul-weather friend. The fact that housing has slackened during boom periods has taken some of the extreme inflationary pressure off the boom. Equally important, the prompt revival of housing during recessions has made our postwar recessions much less severe than they might otherwise have been. From the point of view of the housing industry, its instability has caused serious problems; but from the point of view of the overall economy, it has been, at least to some extent, a blessing.

Congress, if one is to judge by its procreation of mortgage credit programs, has decided that some other sector of the economy (but not housing) should bear the brunt of anti-inflationary monetary policy. It has implemented its decision by selective credit policies aimed at sheltering housing. It could have chosen a quite different route: namely, to prevent inflation the medicine could be tight fiscal policy (high tax rates and cutbacks in government spending) instead of tight money. If that were done, interest rates could possibly remain relatively low across the board, and the rate ceilings, being irrelevant, would not interfere with the flow of mortgage funds. In a sense, home-building would be favored by a tight fiscal policy in much the same way it is hurt by a tight monetary policy. (Consumer and government spending would probably be penalized most by a tight fiscal policy, leaving home construction relatively unaffected.)

Congress, in its infinite wisdom, has opted for maintaining tight monetary policy *cum* selective credit programs rather than tinkering with tax rates and government expenditures during periods when anti-inflationary policy is the rule. Perhaps Congress knows something we don't about Fanny Mae and her friends. Or could it be vice versa?

PART VII

International Finance

19

MONEY IN INTERNATIONAL

FINANCE

The United States has had a deficit in its international balance of payments almost every year since 1949, which, as everyone knows, is a Bad Thing. As a result, we have lost a considerable amount of gold, and *this*, it goes without saying, is an even more Serious Matter. We were the proud owners of 700 million ounces of gold in 1949, and now we have only about 275 million ounces left.

What to do?

An international "balance of payments" is an accounting record of all payments made across national borders. For each country, it shows the payments made to foreigners and the receipt of funds from them, in the same way that a family might keep a record of all its expenditures and receipts. Americans make payments to others, for example, when we import foreign goods, buy foreign securities, lend to other countries, build factories on the outskirts of London or in the suburbs of Rome, or travel abroad on our summer vacations. On the other side of the ledger, we take in money when foreigners pay us for our exports, buy our stocks or bonds, or visit the Grand Canyon.

A deficit in our balance of payments is no different from a deficit in a household's budget. It means that we have been paying out more money abroad than we have been taking in, possibly because we have been importing more than we have been exporting, or because more Americans are visiting Paris and London than foreign tourists are taking in the sights of Keokuk and Kalamazoo. Foreigners thereby accumulate more dollars than they need for their payments to us, and in the ordinary course of events—at least prior to 15 August 1971—many of these dollars were presented to the United States Treasury with a polite but firm request that they be exchanged for gold. You and I have not been able to get gold for our dollars since 1933, but until 15 August 1971 the Treasury stood ready to promptly if not happily honor all official foreign requests at the rate of one ounce of gold for every $35 tendered. On that date President Nixon got tired of paying out so much gold and called the whole deal off.

Contrary to popular impression, by the way, the price of gold is not ordained by God. The old price of $35 an ounce was arbitrarily set in 1934 by Franklin Delano Roosevelt (who, regardless of what you may have heard, was not the Deity). The new price of $38 an ounce was set just as arbitrarily in early 1972 by Richard Milhous Nixon (who certainly is not).

With 700 million ounces in Fort Knox, Kentucky, valued at $35 an ounce, we owned about $25 billion worth of gold in 1949. The 275 million ounces we still have left, at $38 an ounce, is worth much less—only about $10.5 billion. An obvious way to recoup our losses would be to *really* raise the price of gold—say to $90 an ounce. We would then—presto!—have $25 billion worth of gold once again. In fact, if every country followed our imaginative leadership and raised the price of gold along with us, then *everyone* could have more gold. This would make the whole world richer overnight and automatically solve what is known as the international liquidity problem, a subject on which we will have more sage observations in Chapter 21.

In financial circles, unfortunately, this is known as Bad Thinking. It is called Devaluation, and it is to High Finance what Sex was to Victorian England: a little bit might be tolerated on rare occasions, but to contemplate doing it on purpose is Degrading. Although there may be some misguided souls who might be willing to suffer a degree of degradation for the sake of a $15 billion windfall, a succession of presidents, secretaries of the Treasury, Federal Reserve chairmen, and other Recognized Authorities have assured the rest of us that under no circumstances would they subject the American people to such an indignity.

In any event, while drastic devaluation might restore the value of our gold hoard, it would not necessarily affect our chronic balance-of-payments deficit—the fact that every year we pay out more than we take in. One remedy to cure that situation, a remedy invariably proposed by many in the international financial community and occasionally echoed by some here at home, is the old-fashioned hickory stick treatment.

The Discipline of the Balance of Payments

Balance-of-payments disciplinarians believe that to spare the rod is to spoil the child. Their recommendations as to how we should go about restoring equilibrium in our international accounts are appropriately strict. The Federal Reserve should administer the hickory stick by contracting the money supply and raising interest rates until tight money succeeds in reducing GNP and lowering wages and prices. It is difficult to estimate how much unemployment this might involve—perhaps 10 percent of the labor force, at a minimum.

With a depression-level GNP, the incomes of Americans would be so low that we would be hard put to afford such "luxuries" as travel abroad and the purchase of so many foreign products. In addition, there would be relative price effects. With lower costs and prices in the United States, foreign goods become relatively more expensive, which discourages Americans from buying so many Volkswagens and Japanese transistor radios, thus reducing our imports. The lower price tags here would similarly encourage foreigners to buy more of our now cheaper goods and services, thereby expanding our exports. Less imports and more exports: we will be paying out less money abroad and taking in more, thus eliminating our balance-of-payments deficit.

At the same time, it is expected that purely financial flows would reinforce these effects. The higher interest rates the Federal Reserve induces here would bring in some foreign money seeking our attractive-yielding securities, and domestic money that had formerly been invested in foreign securities would presumably now return home to buy bargain-priced American stocks and bonds.

This is called Defending the Dollar. Obviously, it is not a pleasant process, involving as it does tight money to induce heavy unemployment—heavy enough to wring lower wages and prices out of the economy—and a shrinking GNP. It is clear that it is based on the well-known Rocky Marciano Principle, that the best defense is a good offense: we defend the dollar by attacking the economy.

Professor Marciano thus takes his place in the Annals of Economics, right behind Professor Phillips, of Phillips

Curve fame (see Chapter 6); Professors Gurley and Shaw, of Gurley-Shaw Thesis renown (see Chapter 15); and Professor E. J. Finagle, discoverer of Finagle's Law ("Inanimate objects are out to get us"). Of course, like all firm discipline, the Marciano Principle is administered reluctantly and only for our own good. Rest assured, it would hurt the Federal Reserve more than it would hurt the economy; the Federal Reserve said so itself when, on the basis of this sort of reasoning, it *raised* the discount rate from 1½ percent to 2½ percent on 9 October 1931 and then to 3½ percent on 16 October, a few days later. (It might be noted that by 1931 the Great Depression was something more than a speck on a far-distant horizon; GNP had already fallen 25 percent below its 1929 level, and unemployment had already risen to over 15 percent of the labor force.)

Floating Exchange Rates

Another possible cure for a balance-of-payments deficit, one that does not clash so violently with the goals of high employment, stable prices, and economic growth, is to permit greater flexibility in the price of foreign money (or, what amounts to the same thing, in the foreign price of dollars). Currently, one Deutsche Mark costs Americans 31 cents, one French franc costs us 20 cents, one Mexican peso costs 8 cents, and so on. Such exchange rates are fixed by international agreement under the overall supervision of the International Monetary Fund (IMF), an international institution established at the close of World War II.

The IMF's main function is to oversee the stability of exchange rates. It is really unable to prevent unilateral exchange rate alterations when nations individually decide it is in their self-interest to make such changes. But present world monetary arrangements are nevertheless based on a network of agreed-upon fixed (or pegged) exchange rates, supervised by the IMF.

The alternative to the present system of fixed exchange rates would be to unpeg them, and let them float freely from day to day in accordance with supply and demand conditions for each particular country's money. An increase in the *supply* of French francs would lower their price, say from 20 cents to 15 cents a franc; an increase in the *demand* for Mexican pesos would raise their price, say from 8 cents to 10 cents a peso. This is not permitted under existing international monetary arrangements.

A deficit in our balance of payments, remember, means that we are paying out more money abroad than we are taking in. American importers are paying out more dollars for tiny cars and huge radio-phonograph consoles than foreigners need to buy the wheat and ball-point pens that we are exporting to them. Result: an excess supply of dollars is building up in various countries throughout the world.

If exchange rates were free to fluctuate in response to supply and demand, this excess supply of dollars, due to our sending so much money abroad, would depress the price of dollars to foreigners. The dollar would *depreciate* relative to other monies. Instead of the French having to pay one franc to get two dimes, something *less* than a franc would get them that much of our money; instead of the Mexicans having to pay one peso to get eight American pennies, *less* than a peso would be enough to get them 8 cents. Since foreigners could then get the same amount of our money for less of their own, our goods and services would automatically become less expensive for them even though our domestic price tags remained unchanged. After all, it makes no difference to them whether our goods are less expensive for them because our price tags are lower (the Marciano method) or because each United States dollar costs them less of their own money while our price tags stay the same (the flexible exchange-rate method). In either case, our goods are cheaper for foreigners to buy and our exports are likely to expand.

From the American point of view, this depreciation of our money relative to other monies would mean that a French franc would now cost us something *more* than 20 cents, and a Mexican peso would cost us *more* than 8 cents. Since we would have to pay more to get foreign money, foreign goods would become more expensive for us to buy. With foreign products costing us more, because foreign money costs more, our purchases from abroad—that is, our imports—would be likely to fall off.

Thus the end results are the same as though we had gone the Marciano route: less imports and more exports. We would be paying out less dollars abroad because of our lower imports, and taking in more pounds and pesos as we receive payment for our enlarged exports, thereby putting an end to both the deficit in our balance of payments and the depreciation of the dollar. However, we would be achieving these results by letting exchange rates decline while keeping our economy stable, instead of by sending the economy into a nosedive while keeping exchange rates stable.

Freely floating exchange rates would be a sharp departure from existing international monetary arrangements, which pivot on the fulcrum of fixed exchange rates. By and large, most academic economists, both Monetarist and Keynesian, lean toward floating exchange rates. Most bankers and government officials, on the other hand, seem to favor the present system; they argue that floating rates would create so much uncertainty regarding the price of foreign money that international trade would be seriously impaired. Advocates of rate flexibility reply that fixed rates often create so much disruption at home, by forcing countries to adjust their economies instead of their exchange rates, that they seriously inhibit *domestic* trade—that is, the production of goods and services (GNP). Since we have never really had freely floating exchange rates, it is hard to assess the validity of the practitioners' arguments. But so far, at least, they (the practitioners, their arguments, and fixed exchange rates) have had their way.

20

INTERNATIONAL FINANCIAL

CRISES

One thing that present fixed exchange rate arrangements provide in abundance is intermittent crises in world financial markets, tremors that nearly everyone agonizes over although hardly anyone is really quite sure what is going on. Just to say that exchange rates are fixed doesn't necessarily make it so, especially not when forces of supply and demand are constantly impinging on them. It is in the story of *how* they are fixed, in what must be done to keep them from fluctuating, that we find the reasons underlying almost every monetary crisis that has erupted abroad during the past quarter century, as well as the seeds of the Big One that finally exploded both at home and abroad in the Summer of '71.

The Genesis of International Monetary Crises

Remember how floating exchange rates operate? When a country runs a balance-of-payments deficit, its money *depreciates* relative to other monies; its excess of outflows of funds over inflows pumps too much of its own money abroad, and this burgeoning supply leads to a decline in its relative value. In turn, this relative depreciation of its money tends to expand the deficit country's exports, contract its imports, and thereby restore its balance of payments to equilibrium.

But with fixed exchange rates, the process never gets off the ground. By international agreement (under the IMF), a deficit country that sees its money start to depreciate must promptly step in to stop the decline. It does this by buying up its own money, to mop up the excess supply. However, it can't buy up its own money by offering more of the same in exchange—which, as a government, it could simply print—because that's what people are *selling*, not buying. It has to use *other* money to buy up its own, and this other money is called its international reserves.

Traditionally, international reserves have been held in the form of gold, because of its general acceptability. Since the end of World War II, however, most foreign countries have held a substantial portion of their reserves in the form of U.S. dollars, which are usually just about as acceptable as gold in making international payments. They also hold other kinds of "foreign exchange" among their reserves—pounds, marks, francs, and so on—but mostly they hold U.S. dollars. Other nations acquire dollars when we run our deficits and then hold them as their reserves. (We will return to international reserves, both their composition and their aggregate size, in the next chapter in connection with the subject of international liquidity.)

In general, countries use their reserves in the same way individuals and businesses use their cash balances—to bridge temporary gaps between the receipt and expenditure of funds, to tide them over periods when inflows of funds are slack, to meet unexpected or emergency needs.

In particular, with a system of fixed exchange rates, they also use them to intervene in foreign exchange markets whenever the value of their money threatens to slide away from par (its agreed-upon fixed value). A foreign country generally uses U.S. dollars for this purpose, paying out dollars to buy up any excess supply of its own money, thereby preventing it from depreciating relative to other monies. Or, if it is a surplus rather than a deficit country, selling its own money to keep it from *ap*preciating relative to others.

(This means, by the way, that since it is dollars that are the reserves of foreign countries, the United States is in the unique position of not having to intervene itself to keep *its* money from changing in value relative to other monies; since all the other countries are intervening to keep their monies from changing in value relative to the dollar, this automatically prevents the dollar from changing relative to them. Read that again to make sure you are still with us.)

Now let us watch a mini-crisis develop. A deficit foreign country—say Great Britain, for example—seeing its money start to depreciate, promptly steps in to maintain the par value of the pound by paying out its reserves to buy up excess pounds. *But what if Great Britain continues to run payments deficits?* Then it must continue to shell out reserves to absorb pounds. However, its reserves are far from infinite. Sooner or later, when it runs out of reserves, its "defense of the pound" has to come to a halt. When the authorities sense that propping up the exchange value of the pound is becoming too costly, in terms of the drain of reserves, and no end appears to be in sight, *then*, having stopped defending the pound, they start attacking the IMF —to win a decrease in the exchange rate. Great Britain devalues the pound.

Once the financial community senses that devaluation is

a possibility, however remote, it is likely to undertake actions that increase the probability of its occurence. To illustrate with the same hypothetical example: anyone who owns pounds (or liquid assets payable in pounds) and suspects that the pound may be devalued would be inclined to get out of pounds and into some other kind of money—say Deutsche Marks or Swiss francs—until the devaluation has been completed; then, with the same marks or francs, he could buy back more pounds than he originally had. Such "speculative" sales of pounds by private holders must of course also be purchased by the monetary authorities, as they try to prevent the pound from depreciating below par. This puts an added strain on reserves, thereby increasing the likelihood of devaluation, which in turn stimulates renewed "speculative" activity. "Keeping the faith" under such circumstances is all but impossible.

International transfers of short-term funds stemming from fears of devaluation can feed on themselves in this fashion and rapidly build up to the point where they generate massive reserve drains. Such short-term flows of funds include the purchase of Treasury securities as well as shifts of time and demand deposits. Since devaluations are an ever-present fact of life, countries with balance-of-payments deficits are viewed with some suspicion by those who manage large pools of mobile funds—treasurers of multinational corporations, bankers, financial consultants to private investors, and others with similar responsibilities. Indeed, fund managers will often get nervous about holding a country's money as soon as that country's rate of inflation begins to exceed that of other countries, since this is taken as an early warning signal of future devaluation (prices rising more rapidly than elsewhere hurts exports, encourages imports, and thereby invites balance-of-payments deficits).

All of which produces at least one convenient by-product for the monetary authorities *after* they have devalued: they can blame it on "the unprincipled speculators in foreign exchange who mounted a disloyal attack on the [pound] and finally, despite our staunch defense, succeeded in bringing it to its knees."

There always has to be a scapegoat!

The Special Case of the United States

The above recital of a typical European monetary crisis and ultimate devaluation is not unrelated to American experience. Except that where the United States is concerned, the scenario is slightly different because of the unique role of our dollar as a reserve in world finance. As we have seen, the monetary reserves of other countries consist mainly of U.S. dollars; in turn, the reserve behind the dollar consists mainly of gold. Thus the saga of our dollar has been closely intertwined with that of gold.

The par value of the money of other countries is, in effect, defined in terms of their exchange value relative to the dollar; while the par value of the dollar, in turn, is defined by international agreement in terms of its exchange value relative to gold. Thus the term *devaluation* has acquired somewhat different meanings, depending on whether it is undertaken by a foreign country or by the United States. Devaluation for a foreign country refers to a formal lowering of its fixed exchange rate (its par value) relative to other monies. For example, in the British devaluation of 1967, a pound that had been worth $2.80 became worth only $2.40. Devaluation for the United States refers to a formal lowering of its fixed exchange ratio relative to gold. In the American devaluation of 1934, a dollar that had been worth about one-twentieth of an ounce of gold became worth only one-thirty-fifth of an ounce.

If United States devaluation means that one dollar becomes worth a smaller fraction of an ounce of gold, then of course it takes more dollars to buy an ounce. When a dollar was equal to about one-twentieth of an ounce of gold, then about $20 = 1$ ounce; with a dollar equal to only one-thirty-fifth of an ounce of gold, then $35 = 1$ ounce. Thus it has become customary to speak of a devaluation of the dollar simply as a rise in the price of gold.

CRISIS NUMBER 1. The 1960s had hardly begun before rumors erupted that dollar devaluation was imminent— that the United States was about to raise the price of gold. Underlying these reports was the hard fact that we had been running balance-of-payments deficits steadily through the 1950s, thereby supplying dollars to the rest of the world in excess of the foreign exchange we were taking in. Some of these foreign-held dollars were returned to the U.S. Treasury with a request to please exchange them for gold, if you don't mind. As a result, our gold stock—our monetary reserves—dwindled. At the same time, many U.S. dollars were *not* presented for gold; instead, they were held by foreign countries as *their* reserves. But if they *had* been sent in for gold, we would have been hard put to honor them, because by 1960 our short-term dollar liabilities to foreigners had grown larger than our gold stock. We couldn't have redeemed all the outstanding claims on our gold if we had wanted to.

There was nothing secret about these facts, and they quite naturally gave a lot of people reason to suspect that we might very well devalue, thereby automatically increasing the value of our gold stock. As a result, in anticipation of gold soon being worth more than $35 an ounce, in late 1960 a heavy private demand for gold drove its price to $40 an ounce in London and Zurich, where the main free gold markets of the world, open to anyone, are located. (In financial circles this was called a "speculative attack on the dollar" and was widely regarded as un-American.)

Free-market gold at $40 an ounce posed a threat to our gold reserves. Foreign central banks might be tempted to buy gold from the U.S. Treasury at the official price of $35 an ounce and then sell it in London or Zurich for $40. (Others would be tempted too, but the Treasury would sell only to a government or a central bank.) The crisis remained on the front pages until it was resolved early in 1961, when the world's leading financial nations formally established a "gold pool" to hold the price at $35. The central banks of the United States, Britain, Belgium, Holland, West Germany, Italy, France, and Switzerland began to act in concert, as a syndicate, to sell gold to the free market when the price threatened to rise above $35 and to buy it when it started to fall below.

CRISIS NUMBER 2. All of this worked tolerably well for several years, until the gold pool's sales (to keep the price down) started draining so much gold out of their coffers that the central bankers became somewhat disenchanted at the prospect of playing the game much longer. The reason the gold pool had to keep selling, and hardly ever buying, was the same reason it had gotten organized to begin with: persistent U.S. balance-of-payments deficits, feeding dollars abroad, continued to stimulate the same anticipations that had run up the price of gold in the first place.

Under the circumstances, it was only a matter of time before the next crisis. It arrived late in 1967 as the war in Southeast Asia accelerated the flow of U.S. dollars abroad.

The private demand for gold was so great during 1967 that by the year's end the central banks in the gold pool had almost $2 billion less in their gold reserves than they had at the start of the year. So in March 1968, to front-page headlines, they called it quits.

The gold pool was replaced by a two-tier gold system, which is still in existence. This time, the world's central bankers decided to build their own version of the Berlin Wall, separating once and for all the official monetary gold market from its private counterpart. In brief, they picked up what chips were still theirs and went off to play strictly among themselves, with all transactions within the fraternity to take place at the official price of $35 an ounce, agreeing by blood oath not to sell or buy any more gold in the private market. As for the private buyers and sellers, they could do as they wished and could set whatever price they pleased.

Since March 1968 there have thus been two gold prices, the official price, at which all governmental and IMF settlements are recorded; and the free market price, which fluctuates with the tides of private supply and demand. At times the latter has reached as high as $70 an ounce. As long as the two tiers do not deal with each other, nor with intermediaries, there is no necessary relationship between the two prices—they are like bananas and fire trucks.

The two-tier gold system has worked since 1968, but it contains within it the seeds of its own demise: the higher the free market price rises above the decreed official fixed price, the greater becomes the inducement for those governments with relatively large gold holdings to push for worldwide devaluation up to the market price or, alternatively, to consider selling some or all of their gold to the private market, and perhaps get out of the gold game for good. Countries have violated blood oaths for much less.

But one tier or two, United States balance-of-payments deficits continued and even became larger.

Why Did Dollar Devaluation Take So Long?

How could this country continue to run payments deficits for over twenty years and all that while avoid the consequences (i.e., devaluation) that other countries would face were they to try to do the same? As we have seen, Great Britain or France or West Germany would have had to step in much earlier and pay out reserves in order to stop their money from depreciating below par—pay out reserves to buy up excess supplies of their own money. Continued losses of their reserves in this fashion, accelerated by the inevitable transfers of liquid funds into other kinds of money (this is usually called "a flight of nervous money to safer havens abroad" and it conjures up all sorts of visions), would force devaluation upon them within a relatively short time. Surely it could not continue for over two decades!

But the United States was (and is) in a uniquely fortunate position. While other countries can run deficits only so long as their reserves hold out, we can run them indefinitely because our dollars *are* the reserves of others. Thus there has been (and still is) a rather special demand for U.S. dollars that nothing else, except gold itself, can satisfy. As a reserve money, our dollar is utilized by *other* countries, under IMF agreement, to intervene in foreign exchange markets in order to keep the exchange value of *their* money at par relative to the dollar. (This automatically keeps the dollar from changing relative to them, as we have already noted, without the United States having to intervene itself. If the dollar starts to depreciate in relative value, then other countries will find their money *appreciat*-ing relative to the dollar and *they* will step in and sell their own money (buy dollars) to keep exchange rates at their fixed par values. Which is just another way saying that the reserve role of the dollar puts it in a uniquely fortunate position, especially in a world that has fixed exchange rates.)

Nevertheless, even those upon whom fortune smiles risk running out of luck if they push it too far. Until mid-1971, the entire world monetary superstructure was erected on the basic premise that other countries could always come to the U.S. Treasury and exchange their dollars for gold. By the end of 1970, however, that superstructure looked precariously unstable; the U.S. gold stock ($11 billion) had become so much smaller than U.S. short-term Treasury securities and bank deposits owned by foreign central banks ($20 billion), with the differential widening, that it was evident the United States was at long last in danger of running out of *its* reserves.

In light of our diminishing gold reserves, both absolute and relative to our commitments, other countries became increasingly reluctant to hold the additional dollars spewed forth by our payments deficits. But instead of getting smaller, U.S. balance-of-payments deficits grew bigger; as a consequence, worldwide expectations of impending American devaluation grew at an even faster pace, despite (because of ?) repeated official denials that the United States would ever think of such a thing.

By 1970, the view had become commonplace that the dollar was "overvalued" relative to other monies—that is, that at prevailing (fixed) exchange rates a dollar was able to buy too many Dutch guilders, too many West German marks, too many Japanese yen. Or to put it the other way, others could get too *few* dollars for their money. This contributed to our payments deficits by enabling us to import too much (foreign goods were relatively cheap for us partly because foreign money was so cheap) and export too little (foreigners found our goods relatively expensive partly because our money was so expensive).

The particular sequence of events that set off the inevitable explosion was sparked by vast international transfers of short-term funds in 1970 and the first half of 1971, actually at first more in response to intercountry interest rate differentials than to nervousness over imminent U.S. devaluation. International capital movements, whether in response to interest rate differentials or because of expectations with respect to exchange rate alterations, of course contribute to balance-of-payments deficits (or surpluses) just like imports and exports of goods and services. That is, the purchase by Americans of foreign securities or foreign bank deposits, for whatever reason, involves our making payments abroad (like U.S. imports), and the purchase by foreigners of U.S. Treasury bills or deposits in American banks involves our receiving payments from abroad (like U.S. exports). During 1969, short-term money had moved *to* the United States, attracted by the high interest rates here during that tight-money period. In 1970 and 1971, however, with recession in the United States and interest rates lower here than abroad, funds moved back to Europe, contributing to our payment deficits.

Domestic Complications

Intercountry interest rate differentials pose a dilemma for the Federal Reserve, especially during a recession. Should it attempt to *lower* interest rates at home to stimulate domestic spending (and then see the balance of payments worsen as short-term funds move abroad in search of higher yields)? Or should it attempt to *raise* interest rates at home in order to attract funds from abroad, or at least deter funds from leaving, and thereby bolster the balance of payments (but then see the recession worsen as domestic spending is curtailed by high interest rates)? At times, the Federal Reserve's response to this problem has been to try to *twist* the structure of interest rates here at home, lowering long-term rates to encourage domestic business expansion while simultaneously keeping short-term rates up to prevent an outflow of funds abroad.

However, as the Federal Reserve has discovered, it can twist the interest rate structure only so far. Under most circumstances, it simply is not possible to lower long-term interest rates beyond a certain point without dragging short-term rates down with them. The desire to keep short-term rates from falling too far, because of balance-of-payments considerations, has thus checked the vigor of easy money in the past decade. If there is a lesson to be learned from this—and there is—it is not that the Federal Reserve lacks the power to make interest rates whatever it wishes, although that is true enough (as we pointed out in Chapter 7). The more important lesson to be learned from this, the one applicable to international monetary affairs, is that no central bank can conduct an independent, wholly domestically oriented monetary policy within the framework of fixed exchange rates.

International capital movements have been given added impetus in recent years by the rapid growth of Eurodollars. These unusual creatures are deposits in foreign banks, mostly in Europe, that are on the foreign banks' books as payable in U.S. dollars, rather than in the money of the country where the bank is located. For example, Eurodollars are born when an American transfers his dollar deposit in an American bank to a foreign bank and keeps it there *in dollars* (rather than switching to pounds, say, if the bank to which he transfers his money is in England). They are similarly created when a foreign holder of a deposit in an American bank does the same thing, as when an exporter abroad gets paid with a check on an American bank and deposits it in his local bank outside Paris with instructions to retain it as a dollar deposit (instead of exchanging it into the equivalent amount of francs). Or, for that matter, anyone in another country can create Eurodollars by exchanging his local money for dollars and then depositing them in his local bank, with instructions to keep the deposit in dollar form. The original Eurodollar deposit can then serve as the basis for dollar loans by the foreign bank, and if redeposited the process can be repeated, thereby creating additional Eurodollars.

Close to E$100 billion are now on the books of commercial banks abroad, including the overseas branches of American banks, and they represent a particularly mobile pool of interest-sensitive funds. Indeed, old ubiquitous Regulation Q has had a great deal to do with the growth of Eurodollars: the interest rate ceilings on deposits in the United States have induced many corporate and institutional depositors in American banks to shift their deposits to foreign banks, to get higher yields, but to keep them payable in dollars for the sake of convenience.

In the tight-money years 1966 and 1969, when the Federal Reserve was putting severe pressure on bank reserve positions, its policies were partially offset by Eurodollar transactions. Unable to compete effectively for domestic funds because of Regulation Q, American banks borrowed large amounts of Eurodollars from their overseas branches to restore the lending power the Federal Reserve was just as diligently trying to deplete. These Eurodollar borrowings so blunted the bite of monetary policy that in mid-1969 the Federal Reserve imposed reserve requirements on them in an effort to restrain their growth.

The Real Storm

But to return to our unfolding tael (this word is spelled correctly—look it up): the particular sequence of events that set off the inevitable explosion (that brought down the house that IMF built) was sparked by vast international transfers of short-term funds in 1970 and the first half of 1971, at first more in response to intercountry interest rate differentials than to nervousness over imminent U.S. devaluation. These interest-sensitive short-term capital outflows worsened our already weak balance-of-payments position, however, so that apprehension rapidly mounted with respect to possible dollar devaluation. A flight from the dollar ensued during the first half of 1971, including large-scale conversions of Eurodollars into other monies, especially into the "strong" ones more likely to appreciate than depreciate (such as West German marks, Swiss francs, and Japanese yen).

To maintain the fixed par values of their own money, the central banks of these "strong-money" countries had no choice but to buy up the flood of dollars being offered in the market, for that purpose paying out their own money (marks or francs or yen, as the case might be). To give you an idea of the enormous magnitudes involved: at the end of January 1971 foreign central-bank dollar holdings amounted to $20 billion, *already a historic high*; by the end of May, however, only four months later, they had swollen to $32 billion. In only four months, foreign central banks had bought up twelve billion dollars, almost none of which they wanted!

Such an avalanche of dollar purchases by these central banks, like any other open market buying by a central bank, laid the basis for an enormous expansion of their domestic money supply—in most cases contrary to the prevailing monetary policies of the countries involved. Forced to buy up vast amounts of dollars, and shoveling out their own money to pay for them, other countries were rapidly losing control over their domestic money supply. In the process of maintaining the *external* value of their money, they were losing their grip on its *internal* value.

West Germany wanted out first. In early May, after buying up several billions of dollars in the first few days of the month, it ceased its dollar purchases, abandoned fixed exchange rates, and let the Deutsche Mark float to find its own level. Holland did the same. For a short while the crisis seemed to have been weathered successfully. During June and July there was actually a fair demand for dollars, and foreign central banks were able to get rid of about $5 billion of them.

But that turned out to be only the calm before the *real* storm. In the first half of August there was again a feverish rush to convert both ordinary dollars and Eurodollars into other monies—by midmonth, foreign central-bank dollar holdings soared to close to $35 billion, well above the May peak. And then it was, on 15 August 1971, that President Nixon ended the convertibility of the dollar into gold.

Faced with jittery and panic-prone international financial markets, with $35 billion in the hands of foreign central banks, obligated to pay out gold to any central bank that wanted to exchange its U.S. dollars for it, but with only $10 billion of gold left in the Treasury, Nixon announced that the game was over. There weren't enough chips left.

Actually, the termination of the dollar's convertibility into gold caused little disarray in international finance. Everyone had known for the better part of a decade that the commitment of the United States to pay out gold in exchange for dollars was more symbolic than real. If it had ever been put to a real test, it would have ended years

"O.K. The forward rate for marks rose in March and April, combined with a sharp increase in German reserves and heavy borrowing in the Eurodollar market, while United States liquid reserves had dropped to fourteen billion dollars, causing specu-lation that the mark might rise and encouraging conversion on a large scale. Now do you understand?"

Drawing by Stevenson;
© 1971 The New Yorker Magazine, Inc.

before. Fixed exchange rates also went out the window for four months following 15 August. Most major countries joined West Germany and Holland and permitted exchange rates to float, with each country's money finding its own value relative to the others on the basis of supply and demand conditions. And do you know what? International trade did not come to a halt!

But good things, as Clifford Irving said, rarely last. In mid-December 1971, the leading financial nations resurrected fixed exchange rates as part of a "new look" in international financial arrangements. The Smithsonian Agreement—the Smithsonian Institution specializes in very old things—provides that exchange rates, which will continue to be supervised by the IMF, can fluctuate a little more than before, but not much. They used to be able to fluctuate by 1 percent above or below par before a central bank was required to intervene to stabilize them. Now they can fluctuate as much as 2¼ percent on either side of par. The Financial Authorities felt this was such a drastic change it deserved a new name: so from now on instead of calling the rate that is fixed the par value, it will be called the central value. (So what else is new?)

Par—pardon, central—values were simultaneously realigned, to produce an average depreciation of the dollar of about 12 percent against the major trading nations. In April 1971, for example, for 28 cents you could have gotten 1 West German mark or 1 Dutch guilder or 100 Japanese yen. Now it costs you 31 cents to get a mark or a guilder and 32 cents to get 100 yen. This should inhibit U.S. imports, stimulate exports, and thereby help remedy the payments deficit. (William Branson of Princeton concludes, on the basis of econometric studies, that the Smithsonian realignment should improve the U.S. trade balance by about $8 billion a year.)

And also as part of the Smithsonian Agreement, the dollar finally was devalued—from the equivalent of one-thirty-fifth of an ounce of gold to one-thirty-eighth of an ounce. Which means the official price of gold is now $38 an ounce. Except that it's sort of spooky to talk about a price, when there's no buying taking place any longer at that "price."

21

WHAT ABOUT GOLD?

Once upon a time, long ago and far away, the natives of a small island in a remote part of the world had a monetary system of which they were justifiably proud. Although they lacked commercial banks and had no Federal Reserve, they had something many people consider much more important—a monetary standard. It was not a gold standard. But it served the same purpose. It was a rock standard. Near the southeastern edge of the island, on a high cliff, sat a handsome and enormous rock, awesome to behold and thrilling to touch, and it was this that they decided should serve as "backing" for their money.

Naturally, the rock was too heavy, and indeed too valuable, to actually use as a means of payment. Instead, for circulating media itself, corresponding to our coins and dollar bills, they used special clamshells. People had confidence in these because boldly inscribed on them were the words:

Will Pay to the Bearer on Demand One Dollar in Rock

The very fact that this statement was made meant that no one ever demanded any rock. The assurance that it was there was sufficient.

For many years all went well. The economy was simple but prosperous, and those from the Great Civilizations across the sea who occasionally visited the island marveled at its stability and its thriving commerce. The natives were not reluctant to explain the reasons for their prosperity: hard work, thrift, clean living, and, above all, sound money. Sound as a rock.

Unfortunately, one night a severe storm struck the island. The inhabitants awoke the next morning to find the rock gone, evidently hurled into the sea by the furies of nature. Consternation! Panic! Luckily, however, they were saved from the potential consequences—worthless money and economic collapse—by an accident of fate that took place within the week. One of the younger natives, a child of no more than eight or nine, perched on the very cliff where the rock had once been, was looking at a rainbow arching far out over the horizon. Following it down, he suddenly saw—or thought he saw—the rock, fathoms deep, under the water.

After much excitement, it was finally ascertained that on very clear days, when the sea was calm and the sun at a certain angle, some who had especially strong eyes could see it. Those who could not, which included almost everyone, were assured by those who could that the outlines of the boulder were indeed discernible. And so, the backing still there, confidence in the money was restored, and in a short while the island became more prosperous than ever.

Of course, all the outstanding clamshells had to be called in, so that the elders of the community could strike out the words:

Will Pay to the Bearer on Demand One Dollar in Rock

In their place was painstakingly inscribed:

Will Pay to the Bearer on Demand One Dollar
in Lawful Money

Now, if anyone brought in a clamshell to be redeemed, it would simply be exchanged for another clamshell. As it turned out, however, no one bothered. After all, with the backing assuredly there, the money obviously was as good as rock.

Gold at Home

Our own monetary system, of course, has always been much more rational. Until the early 1930s, all of our money was redeemable in gold at the United States Treasury. Every dollar bill, and for that matter every demand deposit as well, actually or implicitly bore the following inscription:

The United States of America
Will Pay to the Bearer on Demand One Dollar in Gold

Then, overnight, it was declared illegal for anyone in this country to have gold in his possession, except for industrial or dental purposes. Accordingly, the inscription on the currency was solemnly, officially, and duly altered to:

The United States of America
Will Pay to the Bearer on Demand One Dollar
in Lawful Money

In 1947, a literal-minded citizen of Cleveland, A. F. Davis, sent the Treasury a ten-dollar Federal Reserve Note and respectfully requested, in return, the promised ten dollars in "lawful money." He received back, by return mail, two five-dollar bills.

Seventeen years later, in 1964, the venerable inscription was finally removed from our currency. All that remains is

"Then it's agreed. Until the dollar firms up, we let the clamshell float."

Drawing by Ed Fisher;
© 1971 The New Yorker Magazine, Inc.

an unpretentious observation: "This note is legal tender for all debts, public and private." Also (in considerably larger type): "In God We Trust."

Pursuing the same theme somewhat further: until 1965 the Federal Reserve was required to hold reserves in the form of gold or warehouse receipts for gold (called gold certificates). The amounts required were 25 percent behind member-bank deposits at the Federal Reserve banks (member-bank reserves) and also 25 percent behind all outstanding Federal Reserve notes (most of our currency). These gold or gold certificate reserves were considered the ultimate backing behind our money, both demand deposits and currency. Indeed, economics textbooks were fond of portraying our monetary system as an inverted pyramid, with a base of gold that supported, above it, a fourfold expansion of member-bank reserves and currency and then, atop that, a further multiple expansion of demand deposits. It was clear to any conscientious reader that without its Atlas-like foundation of gold the entire U.S. monetary system would collapse.

But then, as the U.S. gold stock dwindled from over $20 billion in 1958 to less than $16 billion at the end of 1964, the gold backing behind member-bank reserves was quietly eliminated by Congress and the president on 3 March 1965. Three years later, on 19 March 1968, the corresponding gold reserve against currency was also abolished, just as casually. No one seems to care. The newspapers hardly mentioned it. Is somebody covering up?

All of which raises an intriguing question. There is, we are told, about $10.5 billion worth of gold buried deep beneath the surface of the earth in heavily guarded Fort Knox, Kentucky. Have you ever seen it? Do you know anyone who has?

Why don't you write a letter to the Federal Reserve or the Treasury, tell them you're going to be in Kentucky anyway, and ask them to let you stop by and take a look at the gold in Fort Knox? On second thought, don't bother. We did, and what we got back was a rather chilly reply: "With reference to your inquiry relating to Fort Knox, all the gold is stored in sealed compartments and no visitors are allowed."

Sealed compartments? No visitors allowed? It sounds

more like King Tut's tomb or Count Dracula's crypt than a twentieth century monetary system. A curse on all who shall enter here! Do you *really* believe there is any gold there? Does it really matter?

Gold Abroad: International Liquidity

We seem to have broken free almost completely from our superstitious attachment to gold here at home. We no longer think we are being deprived of our constitutional rights because it is illegal to have gold in our possession, and we appear to be perfectly capable of transacting business without using little gold coins, the kind we had before 1933.

However, the same cannot be said of the world at large. Private citizens still hoard gold in many countries where there is no law against it, and in some countries where there is. And nations do the same, since they continue to settle up their net debts among themselves by playing house with small gold bars of a specified purity and weight. (Each bar, about the size of an ordinary brick, contains 400 ounces of 99.5 percent fine gold, which at $38 an ounce makes a typical bar worth about $15,000.) In fact, you can even see some of this gold. Foreign governments store much of their gold in the basement of the Federal Reserve Bank of New York. A guided tour takes you down to the crypts. You can even hold one of the bars. Curious, isn't it?—we can touch theirs but not ours.

Settling debts with gold is no doubt less harmful than many things nations do to each other, but it is still unfortunate, as well as irrational, if only because there simply is not enough gold on this planet, at least not at $38 an ounce, for it to be a suitable medium of international exchange. Just as too little money within a country can inhibit domestic economic growth, so the scarcity of gold in the world poses a threat to the expansion of world trade if mankind persists in using it as a primary means of international payment.

There is probably about $85 billion worth of gold in existence in the world today (not counting what is imbedded in molars or used in jewelry or industry)—roughly 2¼ billion ounces, at $38 an ounce. Actually, estimates range from 2 to 2½ billion ounces, which at $38 an ounce implies a dollar value between about $75 and $95 billion. So much of the estimating approaches sheer guesswork, however, that one might as well slice it down the middle and settle for $85 billion as a reasonable figure. For instance, none of the communist-bloc nations will reveal its gold holdings; and private hoarders, regardless of their politics, are even more discreet. Furthermore, gold in the form of jewelry, which is not included in the above figures, may actually be held more as a store of value than for adornment. Not to mention the fact that $38 an ounce, the official governmental price, has been well below the free market price in recent years; using the free market price would make the total value of the gold stock correspondingly higher.

The United States has a bit more than $10 billion stashed away (we are told), and other governments and central banks outside the communist sphere have about $34 billion. The Soviet Union is estimated to have official gold holdings somewhere between $5 and $12 billion (most likely in the neighborhood of $10 billion), and other communist countries including China, perhaps $2 to $4 billion. Finally, there are the substantial private hoards secretly squirreled away, some from the dawn of time, by peasants and potentates from France and Switzerland to India, Kuwait, and Tibet. Lord only knows what these amount to, but brave men calculate between $25 and $35 billion, with around $30 billion a likely figure (which includes a couple of billion in private hoards in the communist countries).

This is not really a very large amount of gold on which to erect the entire superstructure of international payments, which is perhaps one reason that superstructure is so shaky. With 2¼ billion ounces in existence, and each brick-size bar containing 400 ounces, that amounts to about 5.6 million bars. That much could fit into 380 railroad boxcars and still leave enough room for 100,000 copies of *Mad* magazine.

Even more important, the annual production of newly mined gold adds to this stock at the rate of only about 8 boxcars a year—about 50 million ounces (not quite $2 billion) emerges annually from the bowels of the earth. About 70 percent of this, sometimes more, comes from South Africa, a little over 10 percent from the Soviet Union, and about 5 percent from Canada, the three largest gold producers. In many years, this is not enough to satisfy all the *nonmonetary* demands for gold, not to mention the monetary ones. Jewelers, dentists, and manufacturers use about a billion dollars' worth a year, and hoarders frequently acquire and then promptly rebury another billion dollars or more. So even though newly mined output adds almost $2 billion to the total supply every year, some years end with *less* gold on hand for worldwide monetary uses than was available when the year began.

Since nations insist on using gold in international exchange, its scarcity has meant a growing shortage of international liquidity. Just as individuals and business firms hold liquid cash to bridge the gaps between their receipt of funds and their expenditures, and to carry them over periods when inflows of funds are slack, so nations also need to hold an internationally acceptable means of payment for similar purposes. Such international liquid cash balances, usually called international reserves, have traditionally been held in the form of gold because of its universal acceptability. With gold so scarce, however, many foreign countries have taken to holding a substantial proportion of their international reserves in the form of U.S. dollars, as we saw in the previous chapter. They acquire dollars when we run our payments deficits, and then they hold them as their reserves (although, as we have also seen, they would just as soon not get *too* much of a good thing).

This means, however, that to a great extent the supply of international money depends on the vicissitudes of the American balance-of-payments position. When we have a balance-of-payments deficit and pay out more money than we take in, international liquidity expands. But were we to correct our payments deficits and start running surpluses, taking in more money than we pay out, international liquidity would dry up—with potential restrictive effects on the volume of world trade.

The fact that many countries hold their international cash balances, their reserves, in the form of dollars instead of gold also explains why we are so reluctant to devalue by a substantial amount—that is, raise the price of gold to say double its present level, or even higher—even though if everyone did so it would ease the gold shortage overnight and automatically augment the supply of international liquidity. If the price of gold were doubled, to $76 an ounce, then there would be $170 billion worth of gold in the world instead of $85 billion, and every year $4 billion would emerge from the earth (preliminary to going back in again) instead of $2 billion. However, those nations that have been holding U.S. dollars instead of gold would be out in the cold. In a very real sense, given the irrationalities of the system, they have been helping us out by holding on to dollars instead of presenting them to the U.S. Treasury and asking for gold. If we doubled the price of gold, those countries would look more than a little foolish. If they ever did want gold, they would then have to pay twice as much for it.

On the other hand, those countries that have always refused to hold our dollars and insisted on gold instead would benefit greatly from devaluation. Their large gold stock, so wisely accumulated, would double in value. Other major beneficiaries, of course, would be the world's leading gold producers, South Africa and the Soviet Union.

Paper Gold?

Until 1970, the only ways international liquidity could be expanded were by mining gold, U.S. balance-of-payments deficits, or a worldwide increase in the price of gold (worldwide devaluation, carried out by the U.S.). Of the three, the most rational, on balance, is probably worldwide devaluation. However, in addition to the objections to this course of action mentioned in the preceding paragraphs, raising the price of gold would also have the serious shortcoming of promoting instead of diminishing the role of gold in world finance.

The two-tier gold price system established in 1968 and the ending of the external convertibility of the dollar into gold in 1971—both discussed in the preceding chapter— have severely ruptured the umbilical cord connecting international finance and chemical element 79. But the attachment has by no means been severed. Many governments are still convinced that, of all possible stores of value, gold is the safest, the least susceptible to manipulation by other governments, and the most likely to appreciate in value over the long pull. The rise in the price of gold on the free markets of London and Zurich in recent years, to well above the official fixed price, only reinforces foreign governments' desire to hold on to what gold they have and to get as much more as they can. General de Gaulle was no doubt articulating the beliefs of more central bankers than would care to admit it when, in 1965, he rhapsodized over the beauty and desirability of gold, which "does not change its nature, has no nationality, and is eternally and universally accepted as the unalterable fiduciary value par excellence."

In fact, of course, gold does indeed frequently change its nature; it can be refined, melted, molded, minted, sweated, and has often been debased. In terms of its nationality, it is no different from hula hoops, turnips, or aardvarks. It is universally acceptable only because of the belief that it will continue to be so. And its value is certainly not unalterable, as recent history dramatically attests. Gold is not a help but more a nuisance, and frequently a considerable handicap, in international monetary affairs, as nations discovered long ago with respect to their domestic finances.

In 1970, the potentially most hopeful step of all, away from gold, was hesitantly taken with the introduction into the world's monetary system of International Monetary Fund Special Drawing Rights (SDRs)—more commonly known as "paper gold." Actually, SDRs were agreed upon in principle several years earlier, at the 1967 annual meeting of the IMF in Rio de Janeiro, but it took two years before international consensus could be reached regarding their details and still another year before they could be implemented. (Only three years of study, debate, discussion, and hassling around the conference table is tantamount, in international monetary circles, to acting on impulse.)

SDRs are a new form of money, usable (only by central banks and governments) to settle international debts in much the same way as gold. But instead of having to be panned, dredged, or mined from the earth, they are created out of thin air—just like demand deposits—by a purely man-made bookkeeping entry. Over $9 billion of SDRs have thus far (through 1972) been made available to member nations of the IMF, for them to draw upon when needed; this is more than all the gold added to monetary reserves since the mid-1950s (most of the gold produced since the mid-1950s has been used for industrial purposes or has found its way into private hoards).

So far, however, SDRs are not "as good as gold," even though they are guaranteed in value on a par with gold. That is, if the price of gold is officially raised, each unit of SDRs automatically becomes worth proportionally more as well. But their use has limitations, which is not true of gold. A nation with plentiful reserves currently running a balance-of-payments surplus, for example, cannot draw on its allotment of SDRs.

The purpose of SDRs is to assist those countries with balance-of-payments or reserve difficulties: a nation with a shortage of reserves, currently running a balance-of-payments deficit, say Mexico, can draw (for free) on its SDR allotment to meet its payments needs. When it receives its SDRs, Mexico can then sell them to a strong reserve position country that is "designated" by the IMF to buy them, say West Germany. In exchange, Mexico will receive Deutsche Marks, which it can either convert into U.S.

dollars or other foreign exchange or use directly in making necessary payments. Countries "designated" by the IMF to buy SDRs, such as West Germany, do not have to accept them above a specified limit.

Thus "paper gold" is, strictly speaking, a misnomer. SDRs are still far from the true equal of gold in terms of general acceptability. Countries "designated" by the IMF to surrender some of their money for SDRs are not nearly so enthusiastic about the transaction as if they had been "designated" to receive gold itself.

It is obvious that if SDRs are to be a success, they will require continued cooperation among nations. Nevertheless, they represent an inching away from mysticism in international monetary affairs, one small step for mankind. Provided they receive tender loving care, they may hopefully grow and prosper; but by any realistic assessment, it does not appear likely that they will soon topple gold from its pinnacle.

Epilogue

22

IS MONEY BECOMING

OBSOLETE?

What might the financial system look like in the year 2000? Buck Rogers and Flash Gordon are passé, Jules Verne is old hat (around the world in *eighty* days), and *1984* draws too close for comfort. The science fiction of yesterday has become the reality of today. An excursion into financial science fiction for the Brave New World ahead should provide a fitting postscript to this book.

The Decline of Demand Deposits

"He spends money," they say, "as though it's going out of fashion." And perhaps money is indeed going out of fashion.

When checkbook money first began to gain popularity in this country, in the nineteenth century, it took decades before people finally realized what was happening. For a long time, checking accounts were not even considered part of the money supply. They were viewed as proxies or substitutes for "real" money, namely hard cash. Somewhere in the vaults of the banks, it was thought, nestled the coin and currency, dollar for dollar, behind every checking account.

As a matter of fact, even coin and currency were suspect. Dimes and dollar bills were considered mere stand-ins for the *really* genuine article—gold coin or bullion. That, and only that, was truly money. Anything less was, like Daylight Saving Time, a violation of the Lord's will.

Today, demand deposits are gradually losing their monetary importance, just as currency did a century ago. Checking accounts still constitute the bulk of our money supply, but the money supply itself has been diminishing in importance in our evolving financial system. Twenty-five years ago, the money supply amounted to half of our gross national product. Fifteen years ago, it was equal to around a third of GNP. Today, it has shrunk to about one-fifth of GNP. We are carrying on more and more business, both financial and nonfinancial, with a relatively smaller and smaller supply of money.

Just as a hundred years ago coin and currency gradually gave way to the convenience and efficiency of demand deposits, so today demand deposits, as we have known them, are gradually giving way to even more convenient and efficient payment mechanisms. The growth of credit cards, for example, has made it unnecessary to write twenty-five checks when making twenty-five purchases. One check, at the end of the month, will do for all. And often that one check is not even needed. Your friendly neighborhood bank can make an automatic debit to your account at regular intervals, relieving you of the need to write even that one check.

If you have your paycheck sent directly to your bank by your employer, and make most of your purchases with that bank's credit card, with payment then settled up at stated intervals by the bank automatically reducing your account by the amount of the charges incurred, you will soon find your check book obsolete.

If we combine the essence of this already realistic payments system with the potentialities of the high-speed computer, magnetic tape storage, remote feed-ins, and satellite transmission, it does not take too much imagination to make a stab at the shape of things to come.

Debits and Credits in the Year 2000

A few decades from now, coins will probably still be with us for inserting into vending machines that we can then shake and bang to release our aggressions. But checks may well have vanished as quickly as they came. Check payment, after all is said and done, is nothing more than a bookkeeping operation to begin with. As a method of information dispersal as to how the books should be kept, checks are—in light of present and foreseeable technology —notoriously cumbersome, slow, unreliable, and inefficient.

More in keeping with the twenty-first century will be a vast nationwide balance sheet and clearing system, in which debits and credits can be rung up virtually instantaneously by electronic impulse. Every individual and every transacting organization of whatever sort will be tagged at birth with a number and a slot on the "books" of a computerized nationwide accounting and payments system, a National Ledger as it were.

Credits and debits to each individual account will be made by the insertion of a twenty-first century version of a credit card into a twenty-first century version of a telephone or teletype. Instead of a written piece of paper instructing a bank to credit this account and debit that one—that is, a check, with its necessary physical routing from place to place—the insertion of a strip of metal into the appropriate receptacle will automatically debit and credit both accounts instantaneously. It should not be too difficult to devise a system whereby the proper code will serve as a means of verifying the validity of the electronic instructions to the Great Master Bookkeeper in the Sky.

Eliminating checks would be only one of the many advantages that would emerge from such a system. All financial assets are nothing more than a representation of someone else's liability or evidence of equity. Current practice, which consists of inscribing same on embossed parchment, has been absurd for at least two generations. There is no need for stocks and bonds to look like Pronouncements of State by King Henry VIII. As everyone is fully aware, a simple computer print-out would do just as well. However, by the year 2000 even that will not be necessary, since it will all be recorded automatically on the magnetic tape of the National Ledger as soon as a stock or bond is issued or a transaction made.

An even more important advantage will be the saving in time and effort currently devoted to keeping the books in a society slowly but surely being inundated by paper work. We are only kidding ourselves if we think we have made much progress in this area since quill pens replaced whatever it was they replaced.

In any event, manpower will have to be saved somewhere to provide personnel for the army of computer repairmen who will in all certainty be busy around the clock answering customer complaints and fixing breakdowns in the equipment. One supply source for repairmen, of course, will be the cadres presently known as the Monetarists. Their hard-learned skills will be obsolete in the twenty-first century. After spending a lifetime accumulating regressions and correlation coefficients to prove that the money supply is the sole determinant of all plant and animal life, what else will they be able to do when money itself becomes no more than a historical *curiosa*?

A National Ledger payments system will be possible in a surprisingly few years. Already its introduction depends more on costs and financial evaluations regarding its profitability than on purely technological considerations. It remains to be seen whether the necessary services will be provided by one firm, by an association of private financial and nonfinancial firms, or by the government, alone or in partnership with private enterprise.

There are obvious advantages inherent in its being a governmental function. For example, as matters now stand, employees of the Communist Party USA are not permitted to receive social security benefits. If they and other malcontents could also be denied access to the National Ledger, and thus barred from making or receiving payments of any sort, the American Way of Life could be made even more Secure.

Implications for Financial Markets

With methods of communication and the dissemination of information perfected to the ultimate degree by the year 2000, in all likelihood financial markets will finally take on the characteristics of the purely competitive markets that economists have been talking about in classrooms since the days of Adam Smith. Instead of simple buy and sell orders, or bid and offered quotations, potential buyers and sellers of financial assets will be able electronically to transmit

complete demand and supply schedules to a central clearing computer, specifying the amounts of various securities they wish to buy or sell at a range of alternative prices.

Of course, this in itself would not be quite sufficient to
meet classroom standards for a purely competitive market,
since among the prerequisites for such a market is that the
participants possess perfect foresight regarding the future
as well as perfect knowledge of the present. But even that
might be incorporated by feeding probability forecasts into
the Giant Maw of the computer. Is it too farfetched to sug-
gest that such forecasts might even involve some of the
parapsychological techniques—like clairvoyance and pre-
cognition—currently under intensive study at some of our
most prestigious universities and on several all-night radio
programs?

Implications for the Economy

The "New Economics," Keynesian or otherwise, will also
mean something quite different in the twenty-first century
than it means today. Monetary and fiscal policy are far too
uncertain in their impact for use in the Century of Efficiency
that will follow the present Century of Progress.

By that time, all assets and liabilities as recorded on the
National Ledger will be subject to increase or decrease by
any given percentage by Executive Order, thereby instantaneously altering the wealth of every individual and every
business firm in the country. If aggregate spending does
not respond promptly in the direction and amount desired,
further asset-valuation adjustments can be fine-tuned until
the reaction on the part of the private sector conforms to
what is deemed necessary to assure the Good Life for all.

Given human nature, this may possibly give rise to the problem of "valuation evasion"—that is, an illegal market in which assets are valued and transactions effected at prices other than those recorded on the National Ledger. The result would be the accumulation of unrecorded wealth for those involved in such dealings. If this gains currency, so to speak, an entire underground financial system—complete with (unreported) deposits, hand-written checks, and a subterranean check-routing network —is likely to spring up in opposition to the more efficient computerized and satellite-supervised official payments system.

The most effective remedy to prevent such undermining of the common welfare would be to bar all participants in Financial Subversion from access to the National Ledger. Practitioners of too-private enterprise would thus be consigned, along with employees of the Communist Party USA, to deserved financial ostracism as Subverters of the National Happiness.

Such a solution would have the self-evident virtue of safeguarding the Sinews of our Efficiency, while at the same time being consistent with the preservation of our Cherished Freedoms.

SELECTED READINGS

Data and Current Comment

A comprehensive source of information on current monetary data, credit conditions, general economic trends, and the policies of the central bank is the *Federal Reserve Bulletin*, published monthly by the Board of Governors of the Federal Reserve System. An annual subscription ($6.00) can be obtained by writing to the board in Washington, D.C.

However, more sparkling comment and analyses are generally found in the monthly reviews of the various Federal Reserve banks. The most useful and interesting are those of the Federal Reserve banks of Atlanta, Chicago, Cleveland, Kansas City, New York (very austere), Philadelphia, Richmond, and St. Louis (Brand X). Each of these banks will put you on its mailing list without charge if you drop a postcard to its Public Relations Department.

Also well worth reading are publications of several private financial institutions, most notably Morgan Guaranty Trust Company's monthly *Survey*, First National City Bank's *Monthly Economic Letter* (the Brand X of the private sector), and Salomon Brothers' annual *Supply and Demand for Credit*. The main offices of all three of these firms are in New York City.

Books on Money and Policy

Two basic money and banking textbooks that are classics in the field are Lester V. Chandler, *The Economics of Money and Banking*, 6th ed. (New York: Harper and Row, 1973) and Eli Shapiro, Ezra Solomon, and William White, *Money and Banking*, 5th ed. (New York: Holt, Rinehart and Winston, 1968).

A standard anthology of readings on money and monetary policy is Lawrence S. Ritter, *Money and Economic Activity*, 3rd ed. (Boston: Houghton Mifflin, 1967). An even better book by the same author, although on a somewhat different subject, is *The Glory of Their Times* (New York: Macmillan, 1966).

Three highly recommended advanced works are:

John G. Gurley and Edward S. Shaw, *Money in a Theory of Finance* (Washington, D.C.: Brookings Institution, 1960);

Milton Friedman and Anna J. Schwartz, *A Monetary History of the United States, 1867–1960* (Princeton: National Bureau of Economic Research and Princeton University Press, 1963);

Thomas Mayer, *Monetary Policy in the United States* (New York: Random House, 1968).

Keynesian ideas all stem, of course, from John Maynard Keynes, *The General Theory of Employment, Interest, and Money* (New York: Harcourt, Brace and World, 1936). A convenient summary of Milton Friedman's views on monetary issues can be found in his *A Program for Monetary Stability* (New York: Fordham University Press, 1960).

Studies of the Financial Sector

Some formal models used to analyze behavior in the financial sector are:

Stephen Goldfeld, *Commercial Bank Behavior and Economic Activity* (Amsterdam: North Holland Publishing Company, 1966);

Albert Ando and Stephen Goldfeld, "An Econometric Model for Evaluating Stabilization Policies," in *Studies in Economic Stabilization* (Washington, D.C.: Brookings Institution, 1968);

"The Federal Reserve–MIT Econometric Model," *Federal Reserve Bulletin* (January 1968);

Frank de Leeuw and Edward M. Gramlich, "The Channels of Monetary Policy: A Further Report on the Federal Reserve–MIT Model," *Journal of Finance* (May 1969);

William L. Silber, *Portfolio Behavior of Financial Institutions* (New York: Holt, Rinehart and Winston, 1970).

INDEX

American Dream, 152
American Federation of Labor, 64
announcement effect, and market interest rates, 109

balance of payments, international: defending dollar, 236; defined, 233; and devaluation of dollar, 235, 249–250, 254–258, 267–268; Eurodollars, 252–254, 255; fixed vs. fluctuating exchange rates, 237–240, 242–244; and gold, 233–236; and interest rate, 251–252; and international liquidity, 264–268; monetary policy and, 235–236; U.S. deficits, 233–235, 250–252, 257; U.S. dollar as reserve, 245–249
Bank of America, 79
bank failures, 197, 202
banks, commercial, see commercial banks
Belgium, and gold pool, 247
big business, and inflation, 65–66
Bigness Complex, 201
blacks, unemployment rate, 71–72
Board of Governors, Federal Reserve System, 40, 91–94, 95, 96–98, 99, 100, 101, 103, 104
bonds, vs. stocks, 180–181
Branson, William, 257
Brimmer, Andrew, 216, 217

Brunner, Karl, 116
budget: deficit vs. surplus, 141, 143–145, 146–148; national, 7
Burns, Arthur F., 59, 96, 121
business spending, see investment spending
Byrd, Harry F., Sr., 157

Canada, and gold production, 266
capital gains and losses, 19
capitalism, and poverty, 81
capital movements, international, 251, 252–253
central bank: foreign, 255; inflation, and money supply, 68, 69; see also Federal Reserve System
Chase Manhattan Bank, 80
checking accounts, vs. credit cards, 27, 276–278
commercial banks: abroad, 253; branching and entry, 199–203; business loans, 115; creation of money, 11–13, 148–149, 160; demand deposits, 9, 10, 11–16, 261–263, 275–278; deposit-rate control, 197–199; and Eurodollars, 252–254, 255; financial intermediation, 182; monopoly danger, 203–204; and mortgage loans, 225; reserve requirements, 13–16, 217; savings deposits, 185

Commission on Financial Structure and Regulation, 203
communism, and poverty, 81
communist countries, and gold holdings, 265
Communist Party USA, 279, 281
computers: and future financial markets, 280–281; and future payments system, 277–279
conspiratorial theory, of interest rates, 78–80
consumer installment loans, and reserve requirements, 217–218
consumer spending, 163, 212, 230; and credit cards, 26–27; and GNP, 38, 141, 145, 209; and interest rate, 35; and monetary policy, 56–57; and taxation, 150, 212–214
Continental Congress (America), and hyperinflation, 60, 62
convenience and needs criterion (banking), 202
cost of living, and creeping inflation, 61–64, 67–69; 1931 vs. 1972, 3–4
cost push inflation, 63–67, 69
Council of Economic Advisers, 30, 83, 103
countercyclical monetary policy, and time lag, 132
credit, availability of, 11; vs. money, and GNP, 35, 38–41
credit cards, vs. checking accounts, 27, 276–278
credit policies, selective, 215–216; drawbacks, 218–219; and housing industry, 216–217, 219–220; and reserve requirements on loans, 217–218
creeping inflation, and cost of living, 61–64, 67–69; 1931 vs. 1972, 3–4
creeping socialism, 8; and poverty, 81
currency: and gold backing, 10; and money supply, 9, 11–12, 117

defense spending (federal), 210, 212; and GNP, 209
deficit financing, 146–148, 158
deGaulle, Charles, 269
demand deposits: vs. credit cards, 27, 276–278; decline of, 275–278; and gold backing, 10; and money supply, 9, 11–13; and open market operations, 15–16; reserve requirements for, 13–14
demand pull inflation, 62–63, 66
Department of Housing and Urban Development, 228
deposit insurance, federal, 197, 202
deposit-rate control, 191–192, 197–199
deposits, private nonbank (RPDs), 117, 125
Depression, Great, 8, 25, 68, 175, 237
devaluation, 235, 238–239, 241–246; defined, 245, 246; and U.S. dollars, 249–250, 254–258, 267–268; *see also* gold
discount rate: announcement effect, 106–107, 109–110; for banks, 14–15; defined, 106; and Federal Reserve, 99, 105–112, 237; and interest rate, 107, 109, 113; and market interest rate, 107, 109–110; as monetary control, 105–107, 109–110; and Treasury bills, 107
discrimination, and poverty, 82
disintermediation, financial, 189–190, 191, 194, 225, 227, 229; defined, 183; *see also* financial intermediation

earnings prospects criterion (banking), 202
easy money, and business cycle, 132–133; and stock market, 179; vs. tight money, 51
Eccles, Marriner S., 96
econometric model, 48; defined, 47

economic activity, and interest rates, 5
economic growth, 210–211; and money, 4, 7; and reordering priorities, 210–211
economic power, of labor unions, 64–65
Economics (Paul Samuelson), 171
Eisenhower, Dwight D., 157; administration of, 30
employment: in construction industry, 221; and money, 4, 9; and taxation, 150; *see also* full employment
Employment Act (1946), 65
Eurodollars, 252–254, 255
Europe, wage-price controls in, 76–77
exchange rate: fixed, 241–246, 252, 257; flexible, 237–240; and Smithsonian Agreement, 257–258
executive branch, *see* president (U.S.)
exports, and balance of payments, 236, 239, 242, 251

Federal Advisory Council, 94–95, 100
federal credit programs, and mortgage loans, 228–230; *see also* credit policies, selective
Federal Deposit Insurance Corporation, 197
Federal Home Loan Bank Board, 190
Federal Home Loan Bank System, 228–229
Federal Home Loan Mortgage Corporation, 228
Federal National Mortgage Association, 215, 228–229
Federal Open Market Committee (FOMC), 95, 96, 98–99, 118, 119, 120–130
Federal Reserve Act (1913), 96, 98, 101, 192

Federal Reserve Bank of New York, 92, 95, 99, 100, 127, 130, 194, 264
Federal Reserve Bank of St. Louis, 40, 48, 50, 51, 125, 150, 152
Federal Reserve-MIT-Penn econometric model, *see* FMP model
Federal Reserve System, 33, 48, 57–58, 80, 125, 160, 174, 185; and announcement effect, 109; automatic increase of money supply, ,133; and balance of payments, 235–236; Board of Governors, 40, 91–94, 95, 96–98, 99, 100, 101, 103, 104; Chairman of Board of Governors, 96, 103; and Congress, 11, 91–92, 93, 95, 101–102, 103; credit vs. monetary policies, 11–13, 39–40; discount rate, 14–15, 95, 99, 105–112, 237; and Eurodollars, 253–254; Federal Advisory Council, 94–95, 100; gold backing for member-bank reserves, 262–263; and inflation, 188; interest rates and balance of payments, 251–252; and margin requirements, 178; member-bank reserves, 111–112; member banks, 92, 94, 98, 100; membership in, 112; and monetary policy, 50, 132–136; and money supply, 21–22; and national debt, 168; and near-monies, 187–188; and open market operations, 15–16, 17, 31–32, 34, 51–52, 53, 95, 99, 107, 113–114, 127–131, 148, 166; policy indicators, 113–119; and president (U.S.), 91, 95, 101–103; Regulation Q, 191–195, 197–198, 253; Reserve Report, 115; and reserve requirements, 13–14, 99, 111–112, 113; and stock market, 172, 178–181; structure of, 92–95; and velocity of money, 23–25; *see also* Federal Open Market Committee (FOMC)

Finagle, E. J., 237
Finagle's Law, 237
financial intermediation: defined,
182–183; deposit-rate control,
191–192; Gurley-Shaw Thesis,
187–188; interest rates, 183–186;
monetary policy, 187–189; and
money supply, 185; and Regulation Q, 191–195
First National City Bank of New
York, 79–80
fiscal policy: defined, 8; Keynesians
vs. Monetarists, 140–141, 147–
152; measuring, 143–146; vs.
monetary policy, 4–5, 8, 17, 30–
35, 147-153, 229–230; and national debt, 168–169
FMP model, 48–51, 52, 53, 55, 56,
57, 117, 151, 226
France, and gold pool, 247
Friedman, Milton, 4, 5, 9, 29, 30,
73, 74, 132–135
full employment: and GNP, 164;
and inflation, 70–74; vs. price
stability, 70–74
full employment budget, 144–145

Galbraith, John Kenneth, 18n, 76
General Accounting Office, 94
Germany, hyperinflation in, 60–61
gold, 250, 269; annual production,
266; backing for U.S. dollars,
245–246, 247, 250, 255–256; and
balance of payments, 233–235;
as currency backing, 261–264;
and devaluation, 235, 267–268;
and Federal Reserve, 262–263;
hoarding of, 265–266; and international liquidity, 264–267; as
international reserves, 242, 247–
248, 266–268; and money, 4,
7–8, 10; nonmonetary demand,
266; "paper," 268–271; pool
(syndicate), 247; price of, 234,
246–248, 258, 265; vs. rock-
backed money, 259–261; world
supply, 265

Government National Mortgage
Association, 228
government securities, *see* open
market operations
government spending, 142, 163,
164, 165; and GNP, 38, 141,
145, 146–147, 149, 150–152,
209; and monetary policy, 56–57
Great Britain: devaluation of
pound, 243, 245; and gold
pool, 247; poverty in, 81
Great Crash, The (Galbraith),
18n
gross national product (GNP), 7,
57, 143, 209; and budget deficit
vs. surplus, 141–145, 146–147;
and deficit financing, 146–148;
and exchange rates, 240; and
full employment, 164; and full
employment budget, 144–145;
and government spending, 38,
141, 145, 146–147, 151, 150–
152, 209; and housing industry,
222–223; and interest rate, 147–
148; and investment spending,
150, 209, 211–212; and monetary policy, 19, 30–38, 49–52,
236, 237; and money supply, 21–
25, 30–38, 140, 148, 150, 276;
and multiplier effect, 141–142,
145; and national debt, 162; and
taxation, 141–142, 143–145, 146
Gurley, John, 187, 188, 237
Gurley-Shaw Thesis, on financial
intermediation, 187–188

Hansen, Alvin, 83, 84
health care, as problem area, 208,
209
holding companies, 194
Holland: and gold pool, 247; money
in, 255, 257
Holmes, Alan, 120, 127, 128, 130
home-building, *see* housing industry

housing industry, 55, 57, 82, 146, 152; and business cycle swings, 221-224, 229; competition for funds, 224-227; and GNP, 222-223; and monetary policy, 221-224, 227-230; and money, 4; mortgage interest rates, 85, 224-227; as problem area, 208, 209; and selective credit policies, 216-217, 219-220
Hungary, hyperinflation in, 60-61
hyperinflation, 60-61, 75

impact lag, in monetary policy, 46, 47, 57
imports, and balance of payments, 236, 239, 242, 251
income, and spending, 141-142
income distribution, 81-82, 162
income maintenance programs, 214
inflation, 3-4, 36, 45, 47, 152, 210, 244; and big business, 65-66; cost push, 63-67, 69; creeping, 61-62; demand pull, 62-63, 66; and employment, 70-74; and fiscal policy, 229-230; and fixed incomes, 59-60; hyperinflation, 60-61, 75; and interest rates, 84-87; during Korean war, 66; and labor unions, 64-65, 66; and monetary policy, 83-87; and money supply, 31, 67-70, 86-87, 134; and national debt, 166; and paper money, 8; and take-home pay, 3-4; and taxation, 150-163; and velocity of money, 188; during Vietnam war, 66; and wage-price controls, 74-77; and war, 61, 63; during World War II, 61, 63
institutional investors, and stock market, 171
interest, on national debt, 161-163, 166-168
interest rate, 114, 236; announcement effect, 109; and balance of payments, 251-252; conspira-torial theory of, 78-80; and deficit financing, 146-148; deposit-rate control, 197-199; and discount rate, 107, 109, 113; and disintermediation, 189-190; and financial intermediation, 183-186; and GNP, 147-148; and housing industry, 224-227; and inflation, 84-87; and investment spending, 35, 53-56, 147-150, 226; market vs. deposit, 189-194, 224-225; Monetarist vs. Keynesian views, 34-38, 127; and monetary policy, 5, 52-53, 116, 118, 193; and money supply, 146-147; and mortgage funds, 224-230; poverty, 81-82; and price of income-earning assets, 18*n*, 19*n*; securities prices, 19; and stock market, 173, 179-180; subsidies, 215; and unemployment, 82-84
intermediation, *see* financial intermediation
International Monetary Fund (IMF) 237-238, 242, 243, 249, 254, 257; Special Drawing Rights (SDRs), 269-271
investment spending, 19, 125-126, 164; and GNP, 151, 209, 211-212; and interest rates, 35, 146-149, 226; and monetary policy, 53-56, 57; and taxation, 213
Italy, and gold pool, 247

Japan: economic power in, 204; money in, 254, 257
Johnson, Lyndon B., 30, 83
Joint Economic Committee (Congress), 83, 135
judicial-penal reform, as problem area, 208, 209

Kennedy, John F., 30
Keynesians, 4, 5, 8, 29-30, 47, 52, 57, 73, 115, 116, 140-141, 172, 239, 280; on credit vs. money,

Keynesians (*cont.*)
38–39, 40–41; and deficit financing, 147–152; and Federal Reserve, 135–136; on interest rates, 34–38, 127; and monetary policy, 33– 35
Keynes, John Maynard, 4, 8, 33
Korean War: and credit controls, 215; and inflation, 66

labor unions, and inflation, 64–65, 66; and monetary policy, 83
laissez-faire policy, 7
law enforcement, as problem area, 208, 209
life insurance companies, 196, 218
liquidity: and central bank, 105; and financial intermediation, 184, 185–186, 187–188; and GNP, 31–34; international, and gold, 264–267; international, and U.S. balance of payments, 267; and money supply, 18–19, 31–34, 187; and spending, 22, 126–127
liquidity index, and banking, 202

Macmillan Committee (England), 106
manpower programs, 75
Marciano (Rocky) Principle, 236–237, 239
margin requirements, on stock purchases, 178
market power, of big business, 65
Martin, Wiliam McChesney, 96
mass transit, as problem area, 208, 209
medical research, as problem area, 208, 209
Meltzer, Allan, 116
Mexico, balance-of-payments status, 270
middle-income families, taxing, 213, 214
military-industrial complex, 79
Monetarists, 4, 5, 8, 29, 47, 51–53,

57, 114–117, 140, 172, 239, 278; on credit vs. money, 38–39, 40–41; on deficit financing, 147–152; and Federal Reserve, 135–136; and interest rates, 34–38, 127; and monetary policy, 30–33; and money supply, 132, 134; and Phillips Curve, 73–74
monetary aggregates, 118, 124–127, 128–129
monetary policy, 11–12; and balance of payments, 235–236; and consumer spending, 56–57; countercyclical, 132–136; credit policy of Federal Reserve, 39–40; defined, 139; discount rate, 105–107, 109–110; econometric models, 47–48; and financial intermediation, 187–189; vs. fiscal policy, 4–5, 8, 17, 30–35, 148–153, 229–230; FOMC directives, 121-127; and GNP, 19, 30–38, 49–52, 236, 237; and housing industry, 221–224, 227–230; impact lag, 46, 47, 57; indicators of, 113–119; and inflation, 83–87; and interest rate, 5, 52–53, 116, 118, 193; and liquidity, 18–19; and national debt, 168–169; and open market operations, 127–131; and profit expectations, 35–36; recognition lag, 46–47, 57; and spending, 23–24, 53–57; and stock market, 172, 177–181; time lag, 45–48, 57–58; *see also* Federal Reserve System
money: creation of, 11–13, 147–148, 160; defined, 9; and gold, 4, 7–8, 10; vs. interest-bearing assets, 26–27; market conditions, 118, 124–125; supply of, in U.S., 9; velocity of, 10, 23–25, 26, 27, 33, 35, 127, 134, 148, 185, 188
money supply: automatic increase of, 134–135; vs. credit, and GNP, 38–40; and currency, 276; and

deficit financing, 147–149; defined, 134; and discount rate, 105–107, 109–110; and Federal Reserve, 14–15; and financial intermediation, 185; and GNP, 21–25, 30–38, 140, 148, 150, 276; and inflation, 31, 67–70, 86–87, 133; and liquidity, 18–19, 31–34, 187; and price level, 4, 9–10; and reserve requirements, 13–14, 99, 111–116; and spending, 50–52

mortgage interest rates, and housing industry, 85, 224–227

mortgage loans: demand for, 226–230; reserve requirements, 216–218

mortgage-rate ceilings, 224–225

"multiplier effect," 141–142, 145

mutual savings banks, *see* savings banks

national debt: advance refunding of, 167–168; financing of, 163–164; and GNP, 162; and income redistribution, 162; interest on, 161–163, 166–168; maturity structure of, 166; and monetary and fiscal policies, 168; as mortgage on future, 158, 161, 163–165; national credit, 158–160, and national wealth, 159–160; per capita, 157; during recession, 164; refinancing, 165–169; retirement of, 150–151; and tax rates, 161, 162, 166

National Ledger: computerized payments system, 277–279; and future economy, 280–281

near-monies, 187, 188

New Left, 79

Nixon administration, 30

Nixon, Richard M., 59, 203, 234, 255–256

open market operations, 15–16, 17, 31–32, 34, 51–52, 53, 95, 99, 107, 127–131, 147, 148; importance of, 113–114; and national debt, 159, 166

par value, and dollar devaluation, 257

Patman, Wright, 84, 86

Phillips, A. W., 71, 236

Phillips Curve, 71–73, 75–77; Monetarists and, 73–74

pollution control, as problem area, 208, 209

poverty, 214; causes of, 81–82

president (U.S.), and Federal Reserve, 91, 95, 101–103

price control, by manufacturers, 65–67

price level: and monetary policy, 5; and money supply, 4, 9–10, 31

prices: 1931 vs. 1972, 3–4; World War II rise in, 61, 63

price stability, vs. full employment, 70–74

prime rate, and discount rate, 110

priorities, national, 207–209; and economic growth, 210–211; and resource reallocation, 211–212; and selective credit policies, 215–220; and taxation, 212–214; and Vietnam war, 210–211

profit expectations, and monetary policy, 35–36

purchasing power, of money (1931 vs. 1972), 3–4

Quantity Theorists, 30

Radcliffe Committee (England), 188

recession: interest rate and, 27; money supply and, 31; national debt during, 164; and spending, 9–10

recognition lag, in monetary policy, 46–47, 57

Regulation Q, 191–195, 197–198, 253

Reserve Report, 115

reserve requirements: for demand deposits, 13–14; as monetary control, 99, 111–112, 113
reserves: commercial bank, 129; international, and devaluation, 242–244; net borrowed, 115; net free, 115–116
residential construction, *see* housing industry
resource reallocation, 211–212
retirement income, 60
Roosevelt, Franklin Delano, 8, 234
Ross, Leonard, 75, 77

St. Louis model, *see* Federal Reserve Bank of St. Louis
Samuelson, Paul, 4, 5, 171–172, 212
savings banks, 196, 198, 203, 225, 227
savings deposits: deposit-rate control, 191–192; growth of, in commercial banks, 185; as money, 9
savings and loan associations, 187, 196, 198, 203, 224, 225, 227; deposit-rate control, 188, 191–192; growth of, 185; portfolio restrictions, 217; tax treatment, 215
school reform, as problem area, 208, 209
securities prices, and interest rates, 19, 35
selective credit policies, *see* credit policies, selective
Shaw, Edward, 187, 188, 237
small business: and investment spending, 55–56; and trade credit, 56
Smith, Warren, 83, 84
Smithsonian Agreement, on exchange rates, 257–258
socialism: creeping, 8; and poverty, 81
Solow, Robert, 29
South Africa, and gold production, 266, 268

Soviet Union: gold holdings of, 265; gold production, 266, 268
speculation: and devaluation, 244–245; on stock market, 178
spending: aggregate, 7, 31, 35, 140; and liquidity, 22, 126–127; and monetary policy, 23–24, 53–57; and money supply, 33, 50–52; and recessions, 9–10; and velocity of money, 68; *see also* consumer spending; government spending; investment spending
state laws, and branch banking, 200–201
stock market: competition from bonds, 180–181; institutional vs. individual investors, 171; margin requirements, 178; market value of all shares, 170–171; monetary policy and, 172, 177–181; and money supply, 4, 172–177; 1929 crash, 174; 1966 credit crunch, 179, 180, 193; 1969 credit squeeze, 179, 194
Switzerland: and gold pool, 247; money in, 254

Taft-Hartley Act (1947), 64–65
take-home pay, and inflation, 3–4
taxation: and consumer spending, 150, 212–214; and deficit financing, 147–148; and employment, 151; and GNP, 141–142, 143–145, 146; and inflation, 150, 163; and investment spending, 213; and national debt, 161, 162, 166; and national priorities, 212–214; 1931 vs. 1972, 3; vs. selective credit policies, 219
technology, and bank size, 201
tight money: and business cycle, 132–133; vs. easy money, 51; and inflation, 82–84, 86–87; and reserve requirements, 111–112; and stock market, 179
time deposits, 95, 192
time lag, in monetary policy, 45–

48, 51–52, 57–58, 132; *see also* impact lag; recognition lag
Tobin, James, 75, 77
trade credit, and small business, 56
transfer of short-term funds (international), and fear of devaluation, 244
Treasury, *see* U.S. Treasury Department
Treasury bills, 26, 130; and discount rate, 107, 109; foreign purchases, 251; and national debt, 165–166; rate for, 52–53, 114
Treasury bonds: and national debt, 165–168; yields on, 180

unemployment: black vs. white, 71–72; and inflation, 77; and interest rate, 82–84; and monetary policy, 236, 237; and price stability, 70–72; *see also* employment; full employment
unemployment rate: and full employment, 144; and prices, 64
unions: and inflation, 64–65, 66; and monetary policy, 83
United States: hyperinflation in, 60, 62; and gold pool, 247; post-World War II inflation, 61; poverty in, 81; *see also* devaluation; U.S. dollars
U.S. Congress, 14, 30, 83, 134, 143, 144, 167, 168, 192, 203, 228, 229, 230, 263; and Federal Reserve, 11, 91–92, 93, 95, 101–102, 103
U.S. Constitution, and powers of Congress, 101
U.S. dollars: and devaluation, 235, 249–250, 254–258, 267–268; as international reserves, 242–243, 245–246, 249; "overvalued," 250–251; *see also* gold
U.S. Senate, 93
U.S. Treasury Department, 11, 15, 103, 129, 160, 165–168, 198; and convertibility of dollar into gold, 234, 246–247, 250, 255

velocity, of money, 10, 134, 148; and creeping inflation, 68–69; defined, 23; and financial intermediation, 185, 188; and GNP, 23–25; history of, in U.S., 25; and interest-bearing assets vs. money, 26; and interest rate, 27; stability of, 23–25, 33, 127
Vietnam war, 151, 208, 247; and inflation, 66; and reordering priorities, 210–211

wage-price controls, and inflation, 74–77
wage-price freeze (1971), 77
wage-price spiral, 61–65, 66–67; and monetary policy, 86–87
wages, and interest rates, as inflationary factors, 86–87
Wagner Act, 64
war, and inflation, 61, 63
wealth, national, and national debt, 160
wealthy, taxation of, 213
welfare system, 82
West Germany, 270–271; and gold pool, 247; money in, 254, 255, 257
World War II: inflation and, 61, 63; and national debt, 165; and velocity of money, 25

DATE DUE

GAYLORD		PRINTED IN U.S.A